The Roman Army

Classical World Series

Aristophanes and his Theatre of the Absurd, Paul Cartledge
Art and the Romans, Anne Haward
Athens and Sparta, S. Todd
Athens under Tyrants, J. Smith
Athletics in the Ancient World, Zahra Newby
Attic Orators, Michael Edwards
Augustan Rome, Andrew Wallace-Hadrill
Cicero and the End of the Roman Republic, Thomas Wiedemann
Cities of Roman Italy, Guy de la Bédoyère
Classical Archaeology in the Field, S. J. Hill, L. Bowkett and
K. & D. Wardle
Classical Epic: Homer and Virgil, Richard Jenkyns
Democracy in Classical Athens, Christopher Carey
Early Greek Lawgivers, John Lewis
Environment and the Classical World, Patricia Jeskins
Greece and the Persians, John Sharwood Smith
Greek and Roman Historians, Timothy E. Duff
Greek and Roman Medicine, Helen King
Greek Architecture, R. Tomlinson
Greek Literature in the Roman Empire, Jason König
Greek Sculpture, Georgina Muskett
Greek Tragedy: An Introduction, Marion Baldock
Greek Vases, Elizabeth Moignard
Homer: The Iliad, William Allan
Julio-Claudian Emperors, T. Wiedemann
Lucretius and the Didactic Epic, Monica Gale
Morals and Values in Ancient Greece, John Ferguson
Mycenaean World, K. & D. Wardle
Plato's Republic and the Greek Enlightenment, Hugh Lawson-Trancred
Plays of Euripides, James Morwood
Plays of Sophocles, A. F. Garvie
Political Life in the City of Rome, J. R. Patterson

Religion and the Greeks, Robert Garland
Religion and the Romans, Ken Dowden
Roman Architecture, Martin Thorpe
Roman Britain, S. J. Hill and S. Ireland
Roman Egypt, Livia Capponi
Roman Frontiers in Britain, David Breeze
The Roman Poetry of Love, Efi Spentzou
Slavery in Classical Greece, N. Fisher
Spectacle in the Roman World, Hazel Dodge
Studying Roman Law, Paul du Plessis

The Roman Army

David J. Breeze

Bloomsbury Academic
An imprint of Bloomsbury Publishing Plc

B L O O M S B U R Y
LONDON · NEW DELHI · NEW YORK · SYDNEY

Bloomsbury Academic
An imprint of Bloomsbury Publishing Plc

50 Bedford Square	1385 Broadway
London	New York
WC1B 3DP	NY 10018
UK	USA

www.bloomsbury.com

BLOOMSBURY and the Diana logo are trademarks of Bloomsbury Publishing Plc

First published 2016

British Library Cataloguing-in-Publication Data
A catalogue record for this book is available from the British Library.

ISBN: PB: 978-1-47422-715-5
epDF: 978-1-47422-717-9
ePub: 978-1-47422-716-2

Library of Congress Cataloging-in-Publication Data
A catalog record for this book is available from the Library of Congress.

Series: Classical World

Typeset by RefineCatch Limited, Bungay, Suffolk
Printed and bound in India

For
Andreas (and Kirsten)
Beccy (and Simon)
Erik (and Birgit)

Contents

List of Figures and Tables   x
Preface   xiii
Acknowledgments   xv
Money, Measurements, and Dates   xvi

Introduction   1
1   The Republican Army   15
2   The Army of Augustus and his Successors   27
3   The Army on Campaign   41
4   The Fighting Tactics of the Roman Army   53
5   The Peacetime Army   73
6   Arms and Armor   101
7   The Army as Builders   111
8   The Late Roman Army   123
Conclusions   131

Glossary   133
Select List of Roman Emperors   135
Suggestions for Further Study   137
Further Reading   139
Index   147

List of Figures and Tables

Figures

1. Map of the Roman Empire   xii
2. A Vindolanda writing tablet   7
3. A diploma recording the retirement of a Roman soldier   7
4. A distance slab from the Antonine Wall   9
5. The Spanish city of Numantia with surrounding siege works   11
6. The reconstructed siege works at Beaune   25
7. Legionary standards   29
8. Syrian archers and clubmen   31
9. The tombstone of M. Favonius Facilis.
10. Trajan addresses his troops   34
11. An ox-cart and mule-cart on Trajan's Column   38
12. Loading tents onto a ship on the Danube   42
13. Marching camps in Britain   46
14. The "tortoise" formation   48
15. An auxiliary soldier fighting   63
16. A cavalryman rides down his enemies   65
17. The headquarters building at Newstead   66
18. The bath house and latrine at Bearsden   83
19. The Crosby Garrett "sports" helmet   86
20. A legionary helmet   89
21. A relief of legionaries from Croy on the   102
    Antonine Wall   103
22. Legionaries, a slinger, and a clubman fighting   105
23. Moorish cavalry   106
24. Legionaries building a fort   113
25. The reconstructed timber gate at Baginton   114
26. The reconstructed stone gate at South Shields   114
27. Artist's impression of a fort   115

28. A soldier's doodle in a quarry   120
29. Carpenters' tools   121

Tables

1. The structure of the legion   2
2. The career structure of legionary soldiers   96
3. The career structure of senators   98
4. The career structure of commanders of auxiliary units   99

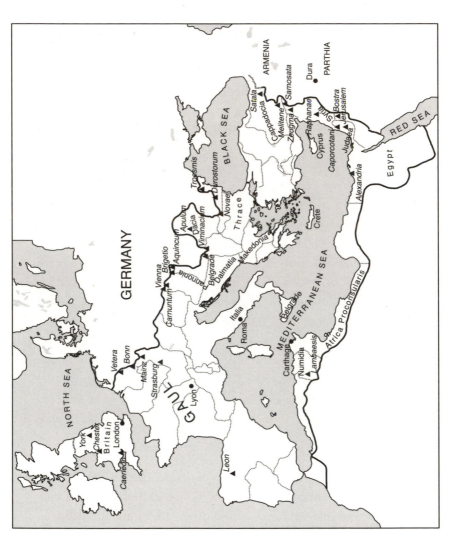

Figure 1 Map of the Roman Empire showing the location of the legions in the time of Hadrian, together with provincial boundaries and certain cities.

Preface

This book was written by someone living at the far north-west corner of the Roman Empire. Yet that corner reflects in its own way the wider Roman Empire because an element of commonality prevailed throughout its length, especially where the army was concerned. For those studying this subject, a two-way process operates: our knowledge of the army of Britain helps us understand the Roman army at large, and the evidence from elsewhere illuminates the army based in Britain.

Many military remains survive from the Roman Empire. These include the Roman temporary camps erected in the second century BC around Numantia in Spain; the Roman siege works at Masada in Israel and Machaerus in Jordan; Roman temporary camps in Britain; and Roman land barriers, forts, fortlets, and towers around the whole of the boundary of the Empire. Rome and other cities contain avowedly military monuments such as triumphal arches, including the Arch of Titus celebrating the victory of himself and his father over the Jews and the Arch of Severus erected in acknowledgement of his many military victories; and columns, including that of Trajan recording his victory over the Dacians and its partner erected by Commodus marking the German wars of his father Marcus Aurelius. On the Lower Danube, in modern Romania, is a further spectacular monument, Adamklissi, though this time in honor of the Roman war dead.

Museums are vital repositories of evidence for the Roman army. Victories were commemorated on coins and on sculpture, such as the remarkable "distance slabs" from the Antonine Wall in Scotland. The more mundane are also of considerable interest. The Vindolanda writing tablets, which can be seen at the British Museum in London with copies at Vindolanda itself, are both ordinary in the way that they reflect day-to-day life on the frontier, yet at the same time offer vitally instructive insights into the operation of the Roman army.

Visits to archaeological remains and to museums are an important way in which we can all understand the Roman army and its operations better.

Acknowledgments

I am grateful to Alan Beale for suggesting that I write this book and Alice Wright for her advice and excellent editing qualities; to Alan Beale, Adrian Goldsworthy, and Lawrence Keppie for kindly reading and commenting on an earlier draft; to Paul Holder for information on the auxiliary forces; and to Michael Bishop for assistance with the illustrations. I am grateful to the following for permission to reproduce illustrations: M. C. Bishop (20); Michael Dobson (5); Angus Lamb (7, 8, 10, 11, 13, 14, 16, 22, 23, 24); Alan Wilkins (6); De Agostini Picture Library, Getty Images (9); The Hunterian Museum, University of Glasgow (4); the Trustees of the National Museum of Scotland (16, 29); Newcastle University (3); the Vindolanda Trust (2); the anonymous owner of the Crosby Garrett helmet per Professor David Ekserdjian (19); 4 is the work of the late Margaret Scott and 21 of Anne Gibson-Ankers, reproduced by kind permission of M. C. Bishop. The remainder are my own copyright.

Money, Measurements, and Dates

The main coin for accounting purposes in the Roman army was the *denarius*. The *as* (sixteen to the *denarius*), however, appears to have been the preferred coin of use on a daily basis. In the Eastern Empire, the Greek *drachma* was used, sometimes even in Roman military records. In the late Empire, the currency was reorganized and a new basic coin, the *solidus*, introduced, technically equivalent to 1,000 *denarii*, but this coin had been greatly devalued from the time of Augustus.

The main unit of both liquid and dry measure of volume was the *congius*, with the *sextarius*, a sixth of a *congius*, widely used in daily transactions; it was equal to about 546 milliliters. An *artaba* was a unit of volume used in Egypt; it was equivalent to 27.13 liters of dry measure.

Note: All dates are AD unless specified as BC.

Introduction

The Roman army was a fighting force renowned to this day for its military prowess and tactical excellence. It created an empire that encircled the Mediterranean and lasted for centuries. When Augustus (reigned 30 BC to AD 14) established the Roman Empire he became commander-in-chief of the army. Though he and his successors retained that authority, and at times took to the field, they appointed provincial governors and legionary commanders to lead their armies and to conduct most of the campaigning on the Empire's frontiers.

The Roman army, like a modern army, comprised regiments of different types. The traditional unit was the legion. At the time of Augustus there were twenty-eight legions, mostly stationed along the frontiers of the Empire. Each consisted of about 5,000 infantry with a cavalry detachment of 120 men. These men were all Roman citizens and served for twenty-five years. Each legion was divided into ten cohorts, each formed of six centuries of eighty men, except the first cohort, which, perhaps only from the 70s, was composed of five double-strength centuries; each century was under the command of a centurion (Table 1). Most of the senior officers of the legion were drawn from the Roman aristocracy, though the prefect of the camp, who looked after logistics, was a former centurion and had risen from the ranks.

The other main branch of the provincial army was the *auxilia*. The auxiliaries were "helpers" to the legionaries, originally provided by the allies of Rome. There were many more auxiliary units than legions; during the reign of Hadrian, there were 566 units totaling more than 200,000 men. By the late first century, there were six different types: the 500-strong regiment, either infantry or mixed

Table 1 The structure of the legion

80 men = 1 century, commanded by a centurion
6 centuries = 1 cohort, which had no commander
10 cohorts = 1 legion, commanded by a legate

infantry and cavalry; the 1000-strong regiment, again either infantry or mixed; and the 500- or 1000-strong cavalry unit—although the terms were only approximate indicators of the size of the units. Auxiliary soldiers, like legionaries, were mostly volunteers, but throughout the Empire some were drafted into the army from conquered tribes. Auxiliary soldiers were not Roman citizens and were only granted this privilege on retirement.

The infantry auxiliary unit was called a cohort and the cavalry equivalent an *ala* (the term means "wings" because in a battle line the cavalry units were placed on the wings of the legions). The infantry were divided into centuries of eighty men and the cavalry into troops of thirty-two soldiers. There was a similar range of junior posts as in the legions.

A smaller regiment was the *numerus*, which simply means "unit". These first appear in the late first century and were probably raised from the frontier tribes. They seem to have varied in size, but they were certainly smaller than normal auxiliary units, and appear to have been commanded by a legionary centurion.

The role of the legions had originally been to spearhead the expansion of the Empire, but when that expansion slowed, their role changed to defending its frontiers. The activities of the auxiliary units and the *numeri*, originally raised to support the legions, similarly changed, as they became more involved in the minutiae of frontier control, preventing raiding, and enforcing the regulations that governed entry to the Empire.

The Roman navy was in reality a military force, differing little from the army apart from the sailors who manned the ships; the sailors were volunteers not slaves. Once the Mediterranean had been pacified, there was little use for the fleets at Misenum and Ravenna in Italy, but the river fleets of the Empire remained an important force helping to protect its frontiers.

The emperor had his own bodyguard, the Praetorian Guard, based in Rome, though it accompanied the emperor on campaigns. The Guard was an infantry unit; the emperor's mounted bodyguard was drawn from the auxiliary units of the frontier areas. There were also three— later five—Urban Cohorts, which served as the equivalent of a police force in Rome. Lyon and Carthage, both the location of a mint, were each assigned an Urban Cohort, though the main role of the cohort at Carthage may have been to guard the transport of corn from North Africa to Rome. Also in Rome was a body of men, the *Vigiles*, whose primary duties were to patrol the streets at night and watch out for fires—in short to be vigilant and, of course, to put out any fires they discovered; occasionally we hear of them acting in a military capacity. Each of the seven cohorts was responsible for two of the regions of the city.

Many army units in the eastern provinces of the Empire were quartered in cities, but in Europe and North Africa they built their own forts. These followed a general plan, though were different in detail. Soldiers were not allowed to marry according to Roman law, but they often took local wives and had families, frequently with their sons joining the army in their turn. These families lived outside the forts where they were joined by merchants, innkeepers, priests, and prostitutes. As soldiers acquired these local ties, it became more difficult to move them, and as a result the army gradually became fossilized on its frontiers.

The commander-in-chief of the Roman army was the emperor. He obviously could not direct day-to-day operations, so he appointed provincial governors to command his armies. He also appointed individual unit commanders, and while governors were allowed to nominate legionary centurions, the proposals had to be approved by the emperor. Some emperors left campaigning to their governors, though it was said of Antoninus Pius in relation to his war in Britain that he directed operations from his palace in Rome rather like the oarsman steers the ship. Others took to the field, including Marcus Aurelius and Lucius Verus, the successors of Antoninus Pius.

The army regularized by Augustus was severely damaged during the civil wars and invasions of the third century. When Diocletian (284–305) took over and restored order, he not only changed the administrative structure of the Empire but he reformed the army. These years saw the creation of new field armies, senior in status to the frontier troops. Another significant change was the move from a primarily volunteer army to military service becoming hereditary or an obligation imposed on local communities who now had to provide recruits.

The crossing of the frozen Rhine by an army and its invasion of the Empire on the last day of 406 heralded the end of Rome's Western Empire. It struggled on until 476, but it had been dealt a mortal blow. The Eastern Empire had suffered a blow a few years earlier with the slaughter of the emperor and his army at the Battle of Adrianople in 378. The Eastern Empire, of course, survived for another thousand years, but the year 400 is a convenient date at which to end this survey.

The sources

One of the significant problems in studying the Roman army is the nature of the sources. We might expect that the great wars of Trajan against the Dacians and the Parthians in the early second century would have resulted in developments in the army, but we have few records of his reign. On the other hand, two historians (supported by inscriptions) provide us with considerable detail about the military activities of his successor Hadrian. There's the rub. Our sources are haphazard in their survival and too often we assign to an emperor such as Hadrian certain changes that might have taken years to have come to fruition, and even then were but a stage in the continuous development of the army. The sources take several forms.

Literary accounts

Our descriptions of the army of the earlier Republic come from the pen of Livy, who wrote at the time of Augustus and therefore narrated events up to 600 years earlier. It is difficult to know how much he understood about the army of that period and how much he interpreted through the prism of the army of his own day, and indeed how much he even understood the army of his own day. That cannot be said of the Greek writer, Polybius, who observed the army at close hand in the middle of the second century BC and wrote a detailed description of the army on campaign.

The greatest account of the Roman army is that of Julius Caesar. His description of his Gallic War fought between 58 and 50 BC, although self-serving, remains the pre-eminent document. Here we see how the army operated in the field, campaigning, fighting, gathering intelligence, and collecting supplies. We can observe how it reacted under pressure and how Caesar maintained morale. Caesar's books are followed in date and importance by those of Tacitus, who described events of the first century AD; the military details, however, have to be extracted from the narrative account of the history of those years. At about the same time another observer, Josephus, a general in the rebel Jewish army who transferred his loyalties to the Romans, wrote an account of the Jewish uprising of 68–73. An outsider like Polybius, his history of the war includes descriptions of the Roman army, with valuable details such as how the army marched.

We are fortunate to possess two books by Arrian, governor of Cappadocia under Hadrian. Arrian's account of his campaign against the Alani and description of his inspection of the military bases round the eastern shore of the Black Sea are valuable because they were written by a serving officer. A hundred years later, Cassius Dio, a Roman senator and consul, wrote a *History of Rome*. It is important not just as the account of a man close to the center of affairs—he also served as a provincial governor—but for his descriptions of battles and his comments on military strategy. For the fourth century, there is the incomparable

Ammianus Marcellinus, an army officer, who left an account of the military events of his time, with excellent descriptions of the army in action.

Two later books on the army also survive, one by Vegetius on military tactics and the other by an anonymous writer generally referred to as pseudo-Hyginus, who wrote a treatise on the army. The former certainly dates to the late fourth century and is written as an encouragement to the emperor of the day to return to "traditional" military practices, while the date of the latter has variously been ascribed to the second or the fourth century. The problem with both is that the dates of the military activities they describe are not clear.

Random information on the Roman army appears in the writings of many authors, including satirists and poets. This is partly because the army was so integral to the Roman state and so many writers had experiences of service within its ranks.

Documents

A further major written source of evidence lies in the surviving military documents. Written on metal, parchment, papyri or wooden tablets, they record the day-to-day activities of Roman soldiers. The range of documents is considerable and includes duty rosters, personnel files on men and horses, daily and annual returns, purchase orders and receipts for purchases, letters soliciting favors as well as letters to and from home, and records of discharge. Documents written on organic materials first came to light in the Near East, particularly during excavations in Egypt and Syria, but wooden writing tablets have more recently been found at Vindolanda and Carlisle beside Hadrian's Wall (Figure 2). Not only do these documents inform us about life on the northern frontier but, through their similarity with the documents from the Near East, they allow us to use the Eastern material with confidence to illuminate military activities on the European frontiers of the Empire. They also include types of documents not previously found; one appears to be a daily report on personnel and equipment.

Figure 2 The front and back of a Vindolanda writing tablet (*Tab. Vindol.* 596). This is a list of apparently random items together with their value given in *denarii* and fractions down to eighths.

Figure 3 A diploma recording the retirement of a Roman soldier. This was issued on July 17, 122 and records the new governor of Britain, A. Platorius Nepos, who is recording building on Hadrian's Wall.

For about 200 years a soldier retiring from an auxiliary regiment, and some fleets, could obtain a military diploma that showed he was given an honorable discharge from the army (Figure 3). To our great advantage, this document carried much additional information relating to the other units discharging soldiers at the same time from the same province, and the date of the event. This helps us build up a catalogue of the units based in each province.

Some writers helpfully provide information on military deployment in the early Empire, but the late Empire offers a unique survival, a list of all its officials arranged in two main sections, the East and the West. The document is known as the *Notitia Dignitatum*. Its great advantage for students of the Roman army is that it not only lists each army commander, but also his regiment and its location. A pattern of military deployment across most of the Empire in about 400 exists in this document.

Inscriptions

Inscriptions provide a vast range of information (Figure 4). These alone often furnish evidence of the existence of regiments and their location and movement. They provide details about the officers and the men. From them we can discover their origins, their age at enlistment, and their length of service. Analysis of the many tombstones and career records has enabled us to chart the career structure of each type of soldier and officer and study its evolution over time. We can thereby determine which careers were normal and which officers were special. Inscriptions are the primary source for the reward structure of the Roman army; we can see which emperors were generous with military decorations and which not. Inscriptions provide information on the gods and goddesses worshipped by the soldiers and their officers, and they are a valuable source of evidence for their wives and families. Inscriptions record the date of the erection of buildings, their names, who constructed them, and sometimes why.

All this material—literary, epigraphic, and documentary—forms but a fragment of the original sources. We have, for example, six strength reports prepared by auxiliary units, yet over 150,000 of such documents must have been submitted to Rome over a period of 400 years. Nor are the returns (and other lists) uniform in the information they provide

Figure 4 One of the highly decorated inscriptions recording the building of the Antonine Wall. This records the titles of the emperor Antoninus Pius, the legionary builder (the Twentieth), and the length of wall that it constructed, 3,000 feet. In the central panel a female, perhaps the goddess *Britannia*, places a laurel wreath in the beak of the eagle, watched by two kneeling, bound, and captive barbarians.

about the size of auxiliary units. In such circumstances, we have to use our evidence with care.

Sculpture

Written sources are not the only form of evidence. Sculpture, not least the two columns in Rome—Trajan's Column and the Column of Marcus, both recording warfare on the northern frontier—provide vivid depictions of the army in action, fighting and building in particular (Figures 7, 8, 10, 11, 12, 14, 15, 22, 23, 24). Another record of activity on the northern frontier is the great monument at

Adamklissi in Romania, erected to record fighting there in the 80s, and thought to be a memorial to the Roman dead following an invasion of the Dacians. Rather more items of sculpture attest Roman victories, such as the "distance slabs" on the Antonine Wall (Figure 4). Depictions of soldiers regularly appear on their tombstones (Figure 9), providing a realistic depicture of their arms and armor, as well as their standards, symbols of office, and military decorations (not quite medals in our terms).

Sites

The Roman Empire was ringed by its frontiers. In over twenty modern countries, the remains of these frontiers are visible. They include linear barriers such as Hadrian's Wall and the Antonine Wall in Britain, the German *limes*, the Valu lui Traian in Romania, and the *Fossatum Africae* in Algeria, legionary fortresses, auxiliary forts, fortlets, and towers. In many places, forts—or rather parts of forts—and towers have been reconstructed (Figures 25 and 26).

Roman armies on the march constructed temporary camps to protect themselves overnight. The greatest concentration of earthworks relating to such camps is in Wales, northern England, and southern and eastern Scotland. In some cases, the complete circuit of the camp, with its gates, is visible. Other camps were constructed to protect a workforce or for practice.

Visible remains of sieges conducted by the Roman army survive, such as those at Numantia in Spain (Figure 5), Masada in Israel, and Machaerus in Jordan. At Burnswark in south-west Scotland, two siege camps straddle an Iron Age fort, but archaeologists still disagree on whether these were erected in time of war or were part of a military training ground.

The military installations erected by the army provide insight into how the soldiers and their officers lived, while studies of military deployment illustrate how the army defended the Empire in times of war and in peace.

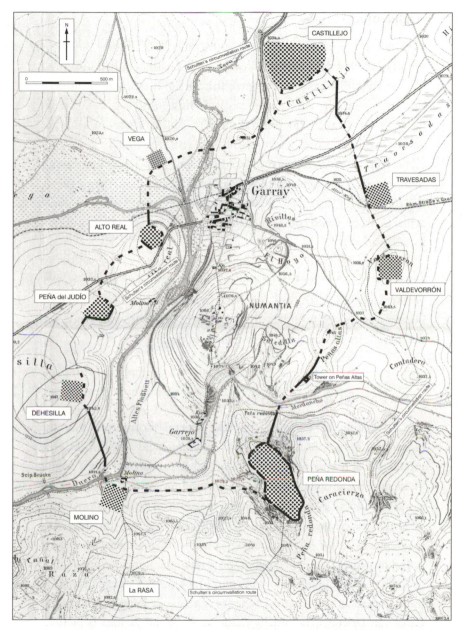

Figure 5 The Spanish city of Numantia (center) with the possible sites of the surrounding Roman circumvallation and camps.

Archaeology

Excavations at military sites started in the nineteenth century, but it was not until the last decade of that century that techniques had improved to the extent that we can recognize this as the beginning of modern scientific research. Archaeological investigations have resulted in the excavation (and sometimes display) of military sites of all types and the collection of a vast date-base of artifacts, which allow us to reconstruct the armor worn by soldiers, and help us to understand more clearly their fighting tactics, as well as the food they cooked, the methods of cooking, and the vessels they used. Study of these artifacts from dated sites underpins the dating of other military installations.

Battles do not usually leave many visible remains but excavations in Germany have taken place at the site of the Battle of the Teutoberg Forest. Here, an earthwork has been uncovered that archaeologists believe was created to hinder the movement of the Roman army, and the investigations have yielded Roman weapons.

Experimental archaeology

The re-creation of the past can take several forms, including the reconstruction of Roman military buildings and earthworks, the production of Roman arms and armor, and re-enactment of past events. These have the advantage of helping us learn how the Roman army went about its business, as well as teasing out the practical details of the making of armor, all elements obscure on both sculpture and the surviving fragments of armor. There is a snag, though—many re-enactments are staged by people not well versed in the ways of the Roman army.

On a personal note, some years ago I took part in an experiment to use a Roman saddle. After many years of research, Peter Connolly and Carol van Driel-Murray finally made sense of the various depictions and remains of Roman saddles and made one, mounting it on a wooden horse. The Romans did not use stirrups; instead, the saddle had horns at the front and the rear. Although no horseman, I quickly was able to learn how to vault onto the wooden horse using the horns as a grip, and to hook my knees under the forward horns and lean to left and right wielding my sword.

Modern research

Finally, of considerable importance to the study of the Roman army is the work of modern scholars who, from the late nineteenth century, have analyzed all the surviving evidence, catalogued it, produced detailed reports and syntheses, continuing their work to the present day, and, in the process, incidentally, shaping our own views of the Roman army. It is not just new excavations and discoveries that enable us to understand the Roman army better, but the meticulous attention to detail of these scholars. Their recording and analysis is important because the conclusions that relate to one Roman province or one unit naturally have a relevance to other provinces within the Empire and other parts of its army. "Evidence by analogy" is an important element in the study of the Roman army.

1

The Republican Army

Roman history is essentially the virtually unique story of a nation trying to catch up with the situations produced by the incredible success of its army.

John Mann

The story of Rome is almost the same as the story of its army. At first Rome was but one of many city-states in Italy, but it gradually gained pre-eminence over them and this was largely achieved through the success of its army. Its army was well armed and well organized, and, after enlistment, its soldiers were trained, though not always as well as they could have been. The organization of the late Republican army can be traced back to one of the last kings, Servius Tullius, at least in Roman tradition. Censuses of Roman citizens were held and the value of their property recorded. The men were then divided by class and assigned to centuries, nominally a hundred strong, though by time of the Empire they consisted of only eighty men. As each soldier had to arm himself, the richest class(es) formed the cavalry with the remainder of the citizens (i.e. the main body) serving as infantry. The first class was well armed, with a cuirass, spear, sword, (round) shield and greaves, but the standard of armor declined with each class so that the lowest was provided with slings or stones only. The system allowed age to be taken into account so that the older men, those over forty-six, did not have the same rigorous duties as their younger colleagues.

This army at some stage, probably around the time it was organized, adopted the Greek method of fighting—that is, in a phalanx with each soldier armed with a long spear and the mass therefore presenting a sort of hedgehog to the enemy. There were eight rows at first, but this was later increased. Importantly, the soldiers fought in close formation so that each soldier helped to protect his neighbor. The phalanx, or proto-legion, reputedly contained 4,000 men, with the cavalry component 600 strong. Yet, this was still an army of farmers who needed time to sow and harvest their crops.

Wars always bring about change, and it was no different in the Roman world. A ten-year struggle against the city of Veii from 406 BC is believed to have led to significant changes. The "legion" was expanded to 6,000 men and the cavalry to 1,800 men. The long Italic shield was introduced, probably first for the less well-armed soldiers. Expenses were introduced: a daily cash living allowance for the soldiers and cavalry horses, together with support for their maintenance.

The end of the war with Veii was quickly followed by an invasion of Italy by the Gauls. As a result of this experience, the Romans changed their fighting tactics, dividing the phalanx into sub-divisions known as maniples. For most soldiers, a throwing javelin replaced the thrusting spear, and an oval shield was adopted, though this was later changed for an oblong version. The new army was more flexible on the battlefield. Now, the first move was to throw the javelins, then to charge the enemy when it was in disarray, fighting with the sword. As Lawrence Keppie has pointed out, these changes "were to be cardinal factors in the Romans' eventual conquest of the Mediterranean world" (*The Making of the Roman Army: From Republic to Empire*, 1998, p. 7).

The next step was to increase the size of the army. By 362 BC, there were two legions and by 311 BC four, probably now numbered, with each consul commanding two of the legions (the two consuls were the chief magistrates of the state; each served for a year and shared command of the army). Each legion had six senior officers called tribunes. These were the closest Rome came to professional army officers, as each had to have five years' service in the army before being appointed.

The legions were supported by troops drawn from the allies of Rome. It seems as though each town provided a regiment of about 500 men under the command of one of their own magistrates termed a prefect. There were also cavalry units, not organized into centuries but into troops. The number of allied soldiers appears to have matched the total of Roman legionaries. The coastal cities subject to Rome provided ships and the men to sail them when necessary.

This is also when we see the beginnings of a military infrastructure with roads constructed to aid the mobility of men and supplies; one of the most famous, the Appian Way leading south from Rome, was constructed in 312 BC. Colonies of Roman citizens, perhaps including retired soldiers, were established to help control newly conquered territory. Several were located on the coast, including Ostia at the mouth of the Tiber, which later became the port of Rome. These cities provided sailors/soldiers for the growing Roman fleet, composed of free men not slaves.

Our main source of information on the army of the Republic, Livy, described the battle formation of the army in the middle of the fourth century BC. There were three main battle lines, with the younger men in the front line and the older men in the rear. In front of the main army was a screen of lightly armed soldiers with a second such group at the back.

This was the nature of the army that faced the Republic's greatest challenge, Carthage, and in particular Hannibal. Rome and Carthage fought two wars, the first from 264 to 241 BC and the second from 219 until 202 BC when it ended with a Roman victory at Zama in North Africa. These wars are perhaps especially remembered for the struggle between Hannibal and P. Cornelius Scipio, known to history as Scipio Africanus, but there were several significant implications for the future of the Roman army—and the Roman state.

Perhaps the most important was the way that Rome, several times defeated, never gave up; here we see the sense of determination that won her an empire. Furthermore, in spite of losing tens of thousands of men, Rome and her allies made good the losses and fought on. By the end of the war, Rome had sixteen legions in the field with men serving for several years; the minimum qualification for service in the army was reduced in order to achieve this. Carthage was a sea power, while Rome was primarily a land power, so to make good the disadvantage Rome created a navy. She not only built ships in number and size to rival the Carthaginian navy, but she invented a new device, a boarding plank known as a raven, which was lowered onto the enemy ship and held fast by a hook on the end so that the Romans could cross safely and fight the Carthaginians on their own ships.

We are fortunate to possess descriptions of the main battles of these wars. Hannibal triumphed at the battle of Cannae, fought in Italy in 216 BC, largely because he understood the standard Roman battle formation, which he used against his enemy, varying his own dispositions to draw the Roman army into a trap where it was surrounded and cut down. After further defeats, the Romans appointed the young Scipio to a special command. Only twenty-four years of age, but battle-hardened, his appointment broke the normal rules for progression up the hierarchy, which were based on age, and thereby presaged the developments of the later Republic.

It may be that it is primarily because these events were so traumatic that we have a detailed description of Scipio's preparations for war. He instigated a training regime that entailed toughening the body, care of the equipment, and use of the weapons. His well-armed, trained, and disciplined army was now ready to face Hannibal. Scipio himself became a superb tactician, as we can see from the deployment of his troops in battle. He learnt from the defeat at Cannae, adopting similar tactics to those of the Carthaginians when he defeated Hannibal's brother Hasdrubal at Baecula in Spain. At Ilipa, also in Spain, he threw the Carthaginian general off balance by changing his order of battle and then undertaking complicated maneuvers that surprised, outflanked, and defeated the enemy.

Scipio's greatest achievement was his victory at Zama in North Africa, in which his training of the army to maneuver on the battlefield was of great importance. Scipio dealt with Hannibal's elephants by leaving gaps in his own line, though masked by light-armed troops. The Roman and allied cavalry attacked the Carthaginian cavalry and chased it off the field. Meanwhile, Hannibal, who had protected his veterans by a screen of allied forces, saw them come under pressure from the Roman legions, which had been re-ordered into a single battle line that pressed forward to engage in hand-to-hand combat. The battle was fiercely fought, but the return of the Roman cavalry tipped the balance in favor of the Romans and the battle was over and with it the war.

Polybius and the army of the second century BC

Our best source for the Republican army is Polybius. He was a Greek politician and army officer, held as a hostage in Rome for sixteen years following the Roman conquest of Macedonia in 168 BC. He was a keen observer of Rome and her affairs, coming to know many Roman aristocrats, in particular Scipio Aemilianus, one of the leading generals of the day, and later accompanying him on campaign. Polybius offers a graphic representation of the Punic Wars and Rome's conquest of Greece, the essential years of her rise to power, within which he provides an account of the Roman army running to twenty-three chapters, in part using earlier Roman sources, now lost. The account covers recruitment, the organization of the legions, the officers, arms and armor, the nature of the camp, and the duties of the soldiers.

When recruiting the army each spring, the first to be elected were the officers. The twenty-four tribunes were required to have had at least five years' military service, some ten years' service; six tribunes were assigned to each of the four legions. When the consuls were ready to create the army, a date was set when all Roman citizens eligible for military service were to report; the assembly took place on the Field of Mars immediately to the north of Rome. The infantry had to serve for no more than sixteen years and the cavalry for ten years before reaching the age of forty-six. Citizens with property below a particular threshold were assigned to naval duties.

The recruits were chosen in rotation by the tribunes until a total of 4,200 had been reached for each legion, 5,000 in times of special danger. Three hundred cavalry were allocated to each legion. One man was chosen to swear on behalf of his comrades that he would obey his officers and carry out their commands to the best of his ability; the other conscripts then did the same. The soldiers chose their own centurions, though the consuls were involved in some way, perhaps in determining seniority. The centurions chose their own second-in-command (called *optio* because the centurion exercised his option) and standard bearers. The cavalry selected their officers in the same way. As described, this seems a complicated arrangement but one may assume that it operated more smoothly in practice, as many soldiers and officers would have fought in several campaigns together and knew with whom they wanted to serve. Such a man was Spurius Ligustinus, whose career was recorded by Livy. Joining the army in 200 BC, he rapidly became a centurion, and over a period of twenty-two years fought in Macedonia, Spain, and Greece, rising to the rank of first centurion and being awarded six civic crowns for his bravery. This man was practically a professional soldier, but he was also a married man with eight children; it was probably the later creation of the permanent Roman army at the time of Augustus that led to the restriction on soldiers getting married.

The soldiers of the legion were arranged in three lines of battle, with a screen of skirmishers in front, each armed according to their duties. The first three rows carried the *pilum*, a throwing spear or javelin, carefully made so that its head bent on impact and it could not be thrown back; it did not only kill and maim, but stuck in shields and rendered them useless. The second row wore plumes to make them appear taller and therefore a more formidable foe. Within each battle line, the basic tactical unit was the maniple, though it was divided into two centuries each with its own officers; three maniples might operate together as a cohort. Once the army was assembled and organized, the men were dismissed and allowed to go home until they were summoned to report for duty (the campaign season lasted from March to October).

One of the most important sections in Polybius' account of the Roman army is his description of the layout of the Roman camp. This always followed a set pattern so that each soldier could find his way round the camp no matter where it was pitched. Surveyors in an advance guard marked the position of tents, starting with that of the general, and roads with flags of different colors. A wide space was left between the tents and the rampart for three reasons: to allow the soldiers to assemble; to provide space for captured cattle and plunder; and to prevent the tents being set on fire by arrows or the soldiers being hit by missiles. Guards were posted at the tents of the consul, by the horses, and at the gates and other important points. A watch-word was chosen for each night and Polybius described the complicated arrangement that ensured that appropriate watch was kept, and the punishment for failure. The severity of the punishment, he stated, resulted in the night-watch being faithfully kept.

Other military failures were also punished severely, in the most extreme case by decimation (literally the punishment of every tenth man), which was carried out by the unfortunates' fellow soldiers usually through clubbing to death. Other punishments included being put on barley rations rather than wheat and forced to camp outside the defenses. To balance these punishments, soldiers were rewarded when they distinguished themselves in battle, each reward relative to the action, with the pinnacle being the gold crown, awarded for being the first over the enemy's walls. In the army of Polybius' time, soldiers were paid and issued with food (forty years later this was extended to the provision of equipment).

Finally, in his account of the Roman army Polybius explained the various ways the soldiers broke camp, depending upon the particular circumstances, such as when they were under threat. Under normal circumstances, the tents would be struck first and the baggage brought together. Then the baggage would be loaded onto the pack animals before the soldiers moved off in a pre-ordained order. Each legion was followed by its own baggage, with the troops of the allies at the front and rear of the column. If threatened, the army advanced in three columns, with the baggage interspersed between them, each outer column being able quickly to turn to right or left to face the threat.

Polybius described the Roman camps on the eve of wars in Greece and Spain. Those in Spain are remarkable because the evidence of a Roman siege still survives in the camps and fortress at Numantia (Figure 5). These Roman camps probably date to the 150s and 140s BC and were erected to protect two legions and an equivalent number of allies. At Renieblas, as many as five camps overlap. One Roman army was forced to surrender here, but a new general, Scipio Aemilianus, the patron and friend of Polybius, reversed the situation, capturing the enemy fortress of Numantia.

We are fortunate to possess a description of the campaign by Appian. He described Numantia being encircled by a wall 2.5 meters wide and 3 meters high, with timber towers at intervals of 30 meters supplemented by seven forts. Excavations have revealed the buildings within some of these forts: lines of barrack-blocks together with administrative buildings and tribunes' dwellings. Numantia illustrates the sheer perseverance of the Roman army as well as its organizational skills. Here were displayed great skills of siege craft, which served the imperial army well in its later wars.

Polybius and Appian provide a view of the Roman army at its zenith. This was the army that within a hundred years was to gain mastery of the Mediterranean basin.

The last century of the Republic

The growth of the Empire brought the rulers—and soldiers—of Rome problems. A constitution that was suitable for a city-state was not appropriate for an empire stretching from one end of the Mediterranean Sea to the other. The speed of Rome's growth also opened up possibilities for its military leaders. The world had suddenly become their oyster; they could conquer new lands almost at will, though some would die in the attempt. In these circumstances, the army itself had to change.

The first of the new warlords was Gaius Marius, a man not from a traditional Roman senatorial family but from a provincial Italian city. In 107 BC, he was appointed commander of the army raised to deal with Jugurtha, King of Numidia in North Africa, seeking success where his predecessors had failed. In order to increase the size of his army, he sought volunteers from those Roman citizens who did not possess property. Although there were precedents for this action, an important threshold was crossed, for these new soldiers had no land and therefore were the makings of a professional force—though legions were still disbanded when no longer needed—and a division between civilians and soldiers. At the end of the war, some of the soldiers were given land in North Africa and settled there.

Victory for Marius was followed by warfare on the northern frontier, in southern Gaul. The Roman army was already well trained, but Marius improved its fitness during a lull in the fighting and another victory was achieved over the Celts.

The career of Marius was significant in that it followed the precedent set by Scipio Africanus, that of early advancement to the most senior posts. He was not only appointed consul *in absentia*, which was illegal, but went on to hold the consulship seven times without the normal break between terms. Marius is also credited with several military reforms. It is, however, difficult to ascertain whether this was the case or whether his fame led to the reforms being accredited to him. Lawrence Keppie has emphasized that the basic structure of the army and its procedures were maintained. Perhaps Marius merely speeded changes already in progress.

Whatever the precise date and whoever the particular initiator of the reforms, we can perceive the legion at this time. It comprised ten cohorts formed of six centuries of eighty men each. At this time also, perhaps, the lightly armed soldiers who operated in front of the main first line of battle were disbanded and probably incorporated into the centuries. The legionaries were now uniformly armed and equipped with both arms and armor being provided by state-owned arms factories. The main weapons were the *pilum*, the throwing spear, now improved by Marius, and the *gladius*, the short stabbing sword, supplemented by a dagger; the soldiers were also protected by a large rectangular shield, which at some stage replaced the round shield formerly carried by some soldiers. The soldiers of Marius, nicknamed Marius' mules, were required to carry their own emergency rations and essential equipment in a bag tied to the end of a forked stick resting on their shoulder. Another innovation dating to this time was the focus on the eagle as the main standard of the legion, the importance of which is clear in Caesar's writings.

Another war in 90 BC, known as the Social War, was fought between Rome and her Italian allies (*socii*). It ended with the granting of Roman citizenship to most men of the Italian cities. Now, the legions had a far larger pool from which to draw recruits, and the number of legions was increased to fourteen or more; however, the new recruits were less loyal to Rome. The reverse side of the coin was that there were no longer any allies as such in Italy. So, mercenaries were hired from Crete (archers), the Balearic Islands (slingers), and Numidia (cavalry).

The 80s, 70s, and 60s saw civil war between the supporters of Marius and those of the new rising star, Cornelius Sulla, fought in Italy and in Spain; warfare in Greece, Asia Minor, and the Levant; the rebellion of Spartacus in Italy; and campaigns against pirates in the Mediterranean. All this led to the creation of a permanent army, the greater professionalism of officers and men, and loyalty to the commander rather than the state.

Julius Caesar in Gaul

Julius Caesar was a Roman politician, eventually becoming head of state, but also a military commander of considerable strategic skill. In addition, he was a gifted writer and self-promoter, writing his own account of his campaigning in Gaul from 58 to 50 BC, an account that has important military details scattered throughout.

The Gallic War begins with the construction of a great rampart and ditch to prevent the passage of the Helvetii and ends with the siege of

Alesia. In both episodes, we can see the Roman soldiers as builders. On the former occasion, Caesar constructed the rampart and ditch for a distance of 18 miles (29 kilometers), with men posted at intervals. At Alesia, he created two concentric circuits of defensive works, one looking in and the other out. The defenses were formed of ditches, filled with water where possible, in front of a rampart topped by a palisade and protected by forked branches (Figure 6). And there were towers at regular intervals. Subsequent additions included sharpened posts, pits, and blocks of wood with iron hooks placed just under the surface of the ground. These are among the most elaborate siege works constructed by the Romans. They are, however, a development of earlier Hellenistic siege craft, as was Caesar's artillery.

One is left with strong impressions after reading *The Gallic War*. These include the speed of movement of the Roman army; the need for Caesar to keep it well fed and therefore the requirement sometimes to move out of his preferred line of march to obtain supplies; the way the army protected itself each night by constructing a camp and made itself comfortable in winter quarters; Caesar's battle tactics, including his use of the auxiliaries; and, of course, the sheer scale of the slaughter of the Gauls. There are also other useful snippets of information, including the speed with which the army could throw up siege works or build a

Figure 6 The reconstructed siege works at Beaune modeled on those described by Julius Caesar in *The Gallic War*.

fleet of ships, the use of a flag to summon men to arms, and the psychological importance of the eagle-bearer. Caesar described his councils-of-war, to which the centurions were invited to join the legates and tribunes. This was a sensible move, as the centurions were battle-hardened while the latter were often young noblemen seeking glory and prestige. During his campaigns, Caesar increased the size of his army from four to twelve legions. Some were paid by the state, but others by Caesar himself, partly from the booty acquired in Gaul, though he was later reimbursed by order of the senate. Not all his new recruits were Roman citizens, as he enlisted men from the area north of the Po where the people had an inferior form of citizenship known as "Latin rights".

Some archaeology is associated with Caesar's campaigns. The siege works at Alesia were examined by Colonel Stoffel for Napoleon III (1853–1870), and investigated again in the 1990s. A camp at Mauchamp by the River Maine was identified in 1862 as one of Caesar's camps; it covered 41 hectares. There are two camps at Gergovia, each set on a low hill, one of which covered 36 hectares; during the siege they were linked by two parallel ditches which protected the soldiers.

The last years of the Republic saw the clash of the two greatest generals of the day, Caesar and Pompey. The events are again described by Caesar and are greatly concerned with the maneuvering of the armies and attempts to control food, water, and other supplies. Siege works were once again constructed, at Dyrrhachium in modern Albania where Caesar sought to separate Pompey's army from his point of supply. The defeat of Pompey at Pharsalus in 48 BC was in part due to the creation by Caesar of a confident, well-trained, and disciplined army, battle-hardened during the campaigns in Gaul.

Four years later, Caesar was assassinated and another round of fighting began, first by his heir, later known as Augustus, against the murderers, known as the "Liberators", and then against Mark Antony, who was defeated at the naval battle of Actium in 31 BC.

2

The Army of Augustus and his Successors

*About 500,000 Roman citizens swore the soldier's oath of allegiance
to me.*

The Achievements of the Divine Augustus

Mark Antony killed himself on August 1, 30 BC, and from that date
Augustus had no rival. For the next forty-four years he was the
unchallenged ruler of Rome. It had taken him fourteen years to achieve
this position through two civil wars and much reconstruction was
necessary. The army now at his disposal was enormous and in much
need of regularizing. It was, in many ways, the army described for us in
detail by Polybius over a hundred years before.

The legions

After the defeat of Antony and Cleopatra, Augustus had at his disposal
sixty legions. With each at full strength, pretty much impossible
considering the warfare they had just experienced, the total number of
men would have been about 300,000. It was decided to reduce the
number of legions to twenty-six or twenty-seven—the exact number is
unclear—and settle many soldiers in colonies; about 120,000 men were
dispersed in this way. Inevitably, with so much fighting, the army—both
officers and men—had become more professional.

Deployment of the legions

The pattern of deployment of the legions was not the same as the
more familiar arrangements of, say, the time of Hadrian a hundred

and more years later. Groups of legions were stationed relatively close to each other in unsettled or recently conquered territory, and the patterns changed as Augustus pacified the lands of his new empire. The legionary strength of the Iberian Peninsula (Spain and Portugal) was increased to eight to complete its conquest but then reduced to three, and subsequently to one. The four legions of Dalmatia were located within its interior with none on the adjacent stretches of the River Danube. Legions were placed along the River Rhine to face the threat from Germany, but there were none on the Lower Danube, which appears to have been peaceful at this time. On the eastern frontier, four legions were centered on Antioch at the western end of the main route to and from Parthia, but none as far east as the Euphrates. Egypt, which had been recently acquired but remained volatile, had three legions, while one was regarded as sufficient for North Africa. The permanency of this army resulted in legionary numbers (and titles) being retained, unlike in previous centuries when an army was raised anew each spring. The legions also acquired symbols, including the elephant, the bull, and the capricorn. These often related to their founder: the legions associated with Caesar used the bull, while those raised by Augustus adopted the capricorn (Figure 7).

Organization of the legions

While the legions were permanent in the sense that they were not disbanded at the end of each season, it would appear that they did not have permanent bases. As noted above, eight legions were assembled in Spain with the intention of completing its conquest. Tiberius brought seven legions together for his invasion of Bohemia in AD 6 while the other arm of the pincer movement consisted of five legions, a total force of about 60,000 soldiers. Rebellion in Dalmatia and Pannonia brought an end to this invasion, but the following year Tiberius assembled ten legions and over seventy auxiliary infantry cohorts and sixteen cavalry regiments together with 10,000 volunteers and other supporters at

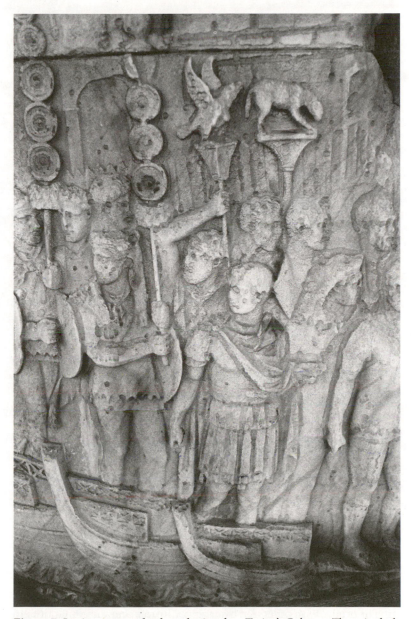

Figure 7 Legionary standards as depicted on Trajan's Column. These include the eagle and a ram, the symbol of the legion I Minervia, which was based in Germany but had been summoned to Dacia to take part in the campaign. The standards behind are probably those of individual centuries. The soldiers are crossing a bridge of boats.

Siscia in order to defeat the revolt. This enormous army was similar in size to the forces operating during the civil wars.

Legionaries still had to be Roman citizens. Augustus fixed their length of service to sixteen years with a further four years in reserve; in AD 5, this was consolidated into a single period of twenty years, followed by several more in reserve. The soldiers received regular pay with a gratuity at the end of their service. This was further regularized in AD 6 through the establishment of a military treasury to provide the money for the end-of-service donative. Although Augustus provided the initial funding, he instituted two taxes—though not without opposition—a 5 percent inheritance tax and a 1 percent tax on auction sales, to provide income for the fund.

In 27 BC, Augustus was given extensive powers, including command over nearly all the provinces that had legions stationed there. As he could not exercise this authority in person, he appointed deputies known as legates. Those that governed provinces were known as legates of Augustus, while commanders of legions were simply legates. These titles, formerly flexibly used, now became permanent and survived into the fourth century: hierarchy replaced flexibility. This reflected the permanency of the army, but also the newly static nature of the Roman state, in which the emperor wished to ensure that he had a cadre of safe and experienced men to run his army and his empire.

The auxiliaries

The auxiliary regiments were reordered under Augustus. We now start to recognize more clearly the units that were later to patrol the Empire's frontiers. There were units of infantry and cavalry, both 500 strong. These were often commanded by a member of the aristocracy of the tribe of origin, with others led by a former Roman centurion. Gradually, both were phased out and command handed over to Roman equestrian officers (that is, members of the lower aristocracy) within a structured career. In the Republic, these units of allies had been provided and paid for by the cities or tribes who raised them; now the Roman state paid their wages.

Auxiliary soldiers were raised from the less Romanized tribes in the frontier areas. Often, newly conquered areas would be required to provide men for the Roman army and these were organized into units named after the new province, hence regiments of Britons and Dacians. Recruitment in these early years was mainly from the original homeland but this was to change, although some regiments, in particular the Batavians, appear to have continued recruitment from home. Auxiliary soldiers at this time appear not to have received any reward on retirement.

Some auxiliary units specialized in certain types of fighting. Gaul, Germany, and Spain provided valued cavalry. Eastern cities such as Palmyra were noted for their bowmen, as was Crete (Figure 8). The Balearic Isles produced slingers. Dio mentioned that twice during the invasion of Britain in 43, a detachment of Germans were sent across the river to attack the enemy because they were accustomed to

Figure 8 Syrian archers and clubmen. The archer carries a composite bow and a sword. The clubmen wear trousers but are bare-chested; they carry oval shields.

swimming in full equipment across the strongest streams. Such skills were neatly encapsulated within the proud boast of a Batavian soldier from the Lower Rhine. On his tombstone he recorded that in front of Hadrian he swam the Danube fully armed and fired an arrow and, before it fell, split it with a second.

The Rome troops

Augustus formed his bodyguard into the Praetorian Guard, which was based permanently in Rome. Its fort was built under Tiberius to the north-east of the city, where three of its four walls can still be seen, now submerged under the later city walls. The Guard contained nine cohorts of 500 men each, one of which was always on duty at the Palace to guard the emperor, armed, but in civilian dress. In view of his closeness to the emperor, the commander of the Guard, the Praetorian Prefect, was a very powerful individual. His men were recruited from Italy and served only for sixteen years. The number of cohorts and the size of each were increased during the civil war of 68–69, but the number soon settled at ten with the size fixed at 1,000 men.

Augustus also recognized the need for other troops in Rome, and so he created the Urban Cohorts, a police force for the city, and the *Vigiles*, who were to deal with the real threat of fire in the city. Together, these formed a considerable body of men: 4,500 (later 10,000) praetorians, 1,500 Urban Cohorts, and 3,500 *Vigiles*. Each was organized into cohorts and the tribunes moved between them, from the *Vigiles* to the Urban Cohorts and finally to the Praetorian Guard. The tribunes had previously served as legionary centurions; in this way, links were created between the different branches of the army. Roman tradition was to keep soldiers outside of Italy, apart from these special troops, and it was not until the time of Septimius Severus (193–211) that a legion was established there. The Second Parthian legion was raised by that emperor to help fight in his Parthian War, but almost immediately was stationed at Albano to the south-east of Rome.

The navy

Finally, now that the whole of the Mediterranean was in his hands, Augustus established two principal fleets, one at Misenum on the Bay of Naples and the other at Ravenna at the head of the Adriatic to ensure safety on the seas. Once piracy had been dealt with, however, these sailors had little to do by way of fighting and some were later sent to look after the awning over the Colosseum in Rome. In the civil war that followed the death of Nero in 68, sailors of the two fleets were formed into two new legions, implying that their existing roles had become redundant.

As the Empire expanded and established its frontiers on major rivers such as the Rhine and the Danube, new fleets were created. The Rhine fleet was established under Augustus. Tacitus recorded that in the late 60s its ships were divided among several forts, though its main base was close to the provincial capital, Cologne.

Tiberius and his family

The move to a professional army was not without its consequences. One was the opposition to the new taxes to fund the military treasury. Another was in response to the conditions of service imposed on the soldiers, which came to a head on the death of Augustus in 14: legions on the northern frontier mutinied. In Pannonia, the soldiers demanded an agreed shorter period of service—some soldiers complained that they had been in the army for thirty or forty years—and the prompt payment of their gratuities. Corrupt and over-harsh centurions were singled out for rough treatment and were beaten up or even killed, including one Lucilius whose nickname 'Get me another' stemmed from his habit of hitting soldiers with his vine stick of office until it broke (Figure 9). On the Rhine, there was a similar situation.

A mutiny was not an auspicious start to the reign of the new emperor, Tiberius, the stepson and son-in-law of Augustus, and one of Rome's

Figure 9 The tombstone of Marcus Favonius Facilis at Colchester. Facilis was a centurion and he carries his vine stick, signifying his rank. © Agostini Picture Library, Getty Images.

most distinguished generals. The new emperor moved quickly to restore order. He sent his son north with two Praetorian Cohorts; the ringleaders were executed and legions moved to new locations. Tiberius' nephew Germanicus was already in Gaul. The situation there was if anything more difficult because the legionaries took over the running of the camp, centurions were murdered, and at first Germanicus had to accede to the soldiers' demands. However, he managed to restore discipline and had the soldiers kill the leaders of the mutiny.

Tiberius reigned for twenty-three years and our view of him is clouded by the second half of his reign when he retired to Capri and left the running of the Empire to his subordinates. Yet his reign did see improvements on the frontier, including the creation of a tow path through the Iron Gates—the great gorge in the Lower Danube between the modern countries of Serbia and Romania—and the tightening of security through the construction of new forts and fortlets. There was also a change that reflected the wider development of the Roman Empire, for he abandoned the attempt to persuade Italians to join the army, preferring to seek recruits from the provinces. Forty years later, the people of northern Italy would react with surprise to a Roman army marching through their countryside, seeing them as uncouth and foreign; this was the new provincial Roman army.

The army was still commanded by Roman aristocrats. The creation by Augustus of a hierarchy of command and a career structure was largely successful, but his successors tinkered with the arrangements. Claudius amended the order in which the commands of auxiliary units and the junior tribunates in the legions were held, and it was changed again shortly afterwards. He conferred the grant of Roman citizenship on auxiliary soldiers on their retirement, together with the right to marry according to Roman law; this had the effect of extending the citizenship to their children. Increasingly, the auxiliary units recruited locally. There was a disadvantage to this, clearly demonstrated during the rebellion of Civilis on the Rhine in 69, when many locally recruited soldiers found that it was easy to transfer their allegiance to the local

aristocratic leader. Fortunately for the Romans, there were few attempts
to break away from the Empire and create independent states.

Vespasian and his successors

The last of Augustus' descendants was Nero, a man with an infamous
reputation. His (assisted) suicide heralded a civil war with four emperors
succeeding each other in quick succession. The eventual winner was
Vespasian, a retired general who had been chosen by Nero to put down
a rebellion in Judaea. Vespasian was lucky to have an elder son who was
an able supporter and serving with him in the East. His second son,
Domitian, who was to succeed his brother in 81, has had a bad press,
but he was an energetic commander on the Danube during serious
troubles later in that decade.

Vespasian had served in the army that invaded Britain in 43. Soon
after his accession in 69, he ordered the army there to move forward
and continue towards the conquest of the whole island. In Germany, he
improved communications by taking land between the headwaters of
the rivers Danube and Rhine, a process continued by Domitian. Both
Vespasian and Domitian continued the trend of moving army units
from the interior of provinces, where they had been placed to control
the new provincials, to the frontiers. But perhaps Vespasian's most
distinctive contribution to the Roman army was the introduction of a
new type of unit, the 1000-strong auxiliary regiment. Under Augustus,
the size of the auxiliary unit had been set at about 500; the new regiment
was about double that size, although the number of men varied between
800 and 1,000. A mixed unit of about 1,000 men formed a formidable
fighting force, the largest regiment after the legion. It may have been
at the same time that the first cohort in the legion was increased in
size from 480 to 800 men, though we have little evidence for the date of
this action. The plan of the legionary fortress at Inchtuthil, dating to
about 84–86, clearly demonstrates the distinctive quarters for the first
cohort.

The army that had developed by the end of the first century continued within this framework for another hundred years and more; it was the stresses of civil wars and invasions from 235 to 284 that brought about the next major changes (see Chapter 8). That is not to say that everything else remained static. The location of the military hotspots changed. Spain had been pacified and its garrison reduced from three legions to one. On the northern frontier, the pressure point changed from the Rhine to the Danube with the resulting movement of legions eastwards. There was also a steady progression away from brigading units together, or in close proximity, in order to mount invasions into foreign territory or protect the Empire from attack. By the 80s, these large army groups had been broken up, the arrangement of brigading two legions together in one fortress abandoned, and both legions and auxiliary units were spread along the frontiers, supplemented by fortlets and towers. This in turn led to a certain amount of fossilization. It became more difficult to move a whole legion of 5,000 men to a new base; the last known example was in the reign of Marcus Aurelius. Instead, detachments drawn from single or several units were dispatched to the war zone, sometimes traveling from one end of the Empire to another. Usually they returned home, but this also was to change and many remained at their new location.

When necessary, Rome could still assemble a large army. Trajan decided to take on the rich kingdom of Dacia in modern Transylvania. In the 80s, the Dacians had wiped out two Roman armies, but Domitian's campaign of retaliation had been halted by an internal revolt. In order to ensure success, Trajan amassed one of the largest Roman armies ever put into the field, 120,000 strong (Figure 10). It included the legion based at Bonn on the Lower Rhine.

War was always the engine for change and affected the structure of command as well as the location of regiments. Major fighting on the eastern frontier in the 160s was followed by over a decade of continuous warfare on the Danube. As in the past, military experience was at a premium, which allowed men such as Tiberius Claudius Pompeianus, son of a knight from Antioch, and the first member of his family to be

Figure 10 Trajan addresses his troops standing in front of a legionary flag and two standards.

appointed to the senate, to rise to the top of the army command and, in his case, marry into the imperial family.

The murder of Commodus in 192 led to a further civil war in which Septimius Severus was the victor. Much of his reign was occupied by warfare, first against his two rivals, and then when they were out of the way, against the Parthians, in North Africa and in Britain; as Herodian said, Severus liked fighting. Severus abolished the Praetorian Guard, which had auctioned the throne after the death of Commodus, and created a new guard with soldiers from the legions. He also founded three new legions, one of which, together with the new Praetorian Guard, was based at Albano 25 kilometers to the south-east of Rome. In effect, Severus had created a strategic military reserve, able to be sent to any frontier, but also serve as the core of an imperial army of invasion. He also increased soldiers' pay and, famously, issued the following advice to his sons: enrich the soldiers and despise everyone else.

The dynasty established by Severus lasted until 235. The unsettled conditions that followed the assassination of Severus Alexander in that year were to bring many changes to the career structure at all levels of the army. Ordinary soldiers with experience and determination could rise through the ranks even to become emperor. And at the lowest level, the careful career planning that gave soldiers appropriate experience before promotion to centurion or decurion cannot be traced later than the 230s. A rather different army grew out of those five chaotic and fateful decades of the third century, something that we will return to later.

3

The Army on Campaign

Famine makes greater havoc in an army than the enemy, and is more
terrible that the sword.

Vegetius, *Epitome of Military Science*, 3, 3

Throughout its history, the Roman state was capable of putting considerable forces into the field. Reputedly, 200,000 men were engaged in the Battle of Philippi in 42 BC when Augustus faced the murderers of his great uncle, Julius Caesar, though it is likely that the legions on both sides were below strength. In AD 6, Tiberius assembled a force of 100,000 to put down the revolt in Dalmatia and Pannonia. An army of this size presented considerable logistical implications as Tiberius realized, and he soon split it up. Such problems were set down by Vegetius in the fourth century:

an army too numerous is subject to many dangers and inconveniences. Its bulk makes it slow and unwieldy in its movement; and as it is obliged to march in columns of great length, it is exposed to the risk of being continually harassed ... The difficulty of providing forage for such numbers of horses and other beasts of burden is very great. Beside scarcity of provisions ... soon ruins such large armies ... and sometimes they unavoidably will be distressed for want of water.

Vegetius, *Epitome of Military Science*, 3, 1

Supplies

Preparations for any campaign began months before any action in the field. There are indications that preparations were in hand for

Caracalla's campaign against Parthia in 217 up to eight months before his arrival in the East. Obviously, men had to be assembled, but so did horses, mules and oxen, and these had to be fed as well as the soldiers.

Gaul was an important source of horses for the army of the Western Empire, but, at the beginning of the reign of Tiberius, after two seasons of fighting the German tribes, Germanicus had exhausted the supply of horses, which may be why he relied more on his fleet in his campaign of 16. Each tent group had a mule for carriage of equipment and oxen were required to pull carts, increasing the pressure for the supply of animals (Figure 11).

In his campaign against Pompey, Caesar sought to prevent his opponent from gathering fodder, an important consideration since Pompey had the stronger cavalry, and he blocked rivers and streams to reduce the supply of water to his enemy. Earlier in the civil war, Caesar was able to prevent fodder, together with water, wood and corn, reaching his enemy's camp in Spain, with the result that after a blockade lasting four days his opponents surrendered.

Many references in Caesar's writings attest his own continuing concern with the supply of his army, and on occasions he suited his tactics to his need to maintain contact with his supplies. In 53 BC, he

Figure 11 An ox-cart and mule-cart on Trajan's Column, both carrying barrels.

delayed his campaign until the start of the harvest. Problems with supplies could threaten the success of a campaign, as Domitius Corbulo found in Armenia in 60: food rations were inadequate, water was short, the summer hot, and the marches long.

Foraging was an important source of supply while on campaign. Caesar foraged for corn in Britain in both 55 and 54 BC, and also in Gaul. He foraged daily, recognizing that if he stayed long in one place he would have to scavenge increasingly further afield, and he protected his foraging parties with cavalry. A later Byzantine writer pointed out that no army should stay longer than three nights in any one place, for in that time it would have eaten all the food in the area and fouled its own water supply.

Julian's army in Persia also foraged, including deer at Dura, destroying what it did not require; however, Ammianus recorded the problems of returning over land that had already been pillaged. Caesar's army took corn both from fields and from settlements, where it was presumably in store, either as food or as seed-corn, and received some in the form of a gift. The collection of corn from fields would imply the carrying of hand-mills by the army. Corn cut at harvest time would be dry enough to use without further drying. Corn cut earlier could have been successfully milled but that did not preclude its earlier harvesting for use as gruel. Caesar noted the awkward time of the year when last year's store of grain had been used up and this year's was not yet ripe.

Food had to be moved. Caesar brought in supplies to his army in the field by land, river, and sea. In 363, Julian supplied his army by ships, which kept pace with the army marching along the banks of the Euphrates; the supply ships were burnt when it was decided to move away from the river. The reasons offered for Germanicus transporting his army by sea along the eastern shore of the North Sea in 16 were that it was out of reach of enemy intelligence and was therefore not vulnerable to surprise attack, it was easier on the men, the campaign could start earlier—and there were insufficient horses available for his army.

Reconnaissance

Care was taken to find out as much information as possible about the land and people ahead in advance of commencing a campaign. Merchants and travellers were interrogated and refugees questioned. Plutarch recorded that in about 80, Domitian commissioned Demetrius of Tarsus to sail to the nearest of the islands around Britain to make enquiries and observations; he recorded that they were sparsely populated and that the inhabitants were all holy men. This visit was exactly at the time that Agricola was campaigning against the Caledonians and it is hard not to conclude that the expedition of Demetrius was related to these campaigns.

On the march the army relied on guides, reconnaissance, prisoners, deserters, and no doubt friendly tribesmen. To aid this work, it used scouts, interpreters, and mappers. Vegetius commented on the need for proper and skilful guides, and he noted that a general knowledge should exist of roads, routes, by-roads, mountains, and rivers. To take but one example, the lines of march of the Roman army in northern Britain indicate a good knowledge of the terrain. In his account of the night attack of the Caledonians on the camp of the Ninth Legion during Agricola's campaigns in Britain, Tacitus remarks that the general learnt of the movement of the enemy from his scouts, implying that scouting took place at night.

The march

Any army of significant size would have taken up a considerable area. Julian's army of 30,000 was 6.5 kilometers long when drawn up ready to march at the beginning of the day, but extended to over 16 kilometers on the march.

According to Josephus, the Roman infantry marched six abreast. Two meters should be allowed for each man, 4.5 meters for a mule and a cavalry horse. Several ancient writers describe the order of march.

Usually, the cavalry was in advance acting as scouts and on the flanks. The legions might march one after the other or in battle formation. Josephus described Vespasian's order of march in Judaea in the late 60s. The light-armed auxiliaries and the archers were at the front in order to scout the route and to prevent a surprise attack. There followed a force of infantry and cavalry and then the surveyors and engineers, placed so that they would be ready to prepare the next camp and improve the roads. The carriages came next, protected by cavalry, and behind that Vespasian himself with his bodyguard. The legionary cavalry led the mules carrying the siege train. Auxiliary commanders and their bodyguards led the legions headed by their eagles, each centurion marching at the rear of his century. Then came the servants of the legions, ahead of the baggage. Finally, at the rear came the soldiers provided by the allies. In 363, Julian purposefully stretched out his army over a distance of 16 kilometers in an attempt to fool the enemy into believing that it was larger than it really was. In the vanguard were 1,500 mounted scouts, the center was formed by the infantry led by the emperor, with the forces of an ally bringing up the rear; the right flank was protected by several legions and the left by the cavalry.

The soldier's burden

Each soldier required food and equipment on campaign. The ration for each soldier was 1.36 kilograms per day according to Polybius, and in addition he ate bacon and cheese and drank wine; oil and salt will also have been required. Meat was eaten when available. Polybius allocated space in his camp for cattle, while Caesar's troops ate cattle and vegetables when other supplies ran out. Several ancient writers stipulate how much food each soldier should have with him. Josephus stated that each carried rations for three days; Cicero that every soldier took rations for more than half a month; Caesar mentions twenty-two days' supplies; the *Life of the Severus Alexander* states that when in hostile territory each soldier usually had to carry rations for seventeen days;

while Ammianus Marcellinus recorded that each soldier on campaign carried seventeen days' rations on his back. One solution to these discrepancies is that that each soldier carried emergency rations that would last three days, while food for up to seventeen or twenty-two days was normally in the baggage train.

Marius, as we have seen (p. 24), ordered that each soldier should carry his own emergency rations and essential equipment, the latter being clarified for us by Josephus, who stated that in addition to the rations for three days, each soldier should carry a saw, basket, axe, pick, rope, sickle, and chain. These were required for felling trees, emptying ditches, carrying turves, foraging, and so on. On Trajan's Column, soldiers marching out to a review carried, on a pole, a metal cooking pot, mess tin, string bag for forage, and a leather bag (perhaps for clothes or water); axes appear elsewhere on the Column. Soldiers on the march on the Column, however, did not carry this equipment; perhaps it had been assigned to the baggage train.

The baggage included tents (Figure 12). These were made of leather, each weighing about 18 kilograms. Eight soldiers occupied each tent,

Figure 12 Loading tents onto a ship on the Danube. This presumably illustrates the transshipment of supplies across the river.

while the officers had their own (though perhaps their slaves slept there as well). There were also medical supplies and artillery. The baggage train also included the soldiers' own possessions. Sabinus' army was thrown into disarray in 54 BC when, during an attack by the Gauls, his soldiers tried to recover their most cherished possessions from the baggage train.

Camp followers also accompanied the army. Scipio Africanus reputedly threw 2,000 prostitutes, together with merchants and priests, out of the camp at Numantia in 134 BC when he took over command of the army; this became such a famous event that it survives in no less than five anecdotes. Both in Gaul and in North Africa, camp followers also accompanied Caesar's army.

The baggage train included two- or four-wheeled carts, pulled by mules or oxen. On Trajan's Column, mules carried tents, weapons (shields and a helmet), and cooking utensils, while two-wheeled mule carts bore auxiliary shields, artillery, tents, and water barrels (Figure 11). Two oxen pull two-wheeled carts bearing weapons (spears and shields) and barrels. The oxen would have slowed the progress of the army. They walk more slowly than mules—a little over 3 kilometers per hour for oxen—and can only work about five hours a day. They require eight hours to feed and then a similar period to digest their food.

Marching camps

Each night the army protected itself by constructing a camp (Figure 13). The outline of the camp and the position of the tents would have been marked out in different colored flags by the surveyors, as Polybius had described. The soldiers then excavated a ditch around the whole of the camp. The ditch was at least 1.5 meters wide and a meter deep, according to both pseudo-Hyginus and Vegetius. The soil was heaped up inside the ditch to form a mound and the two wooden stakes carried by each soldier were stuck in the top to strengthen the defenses. Both authors

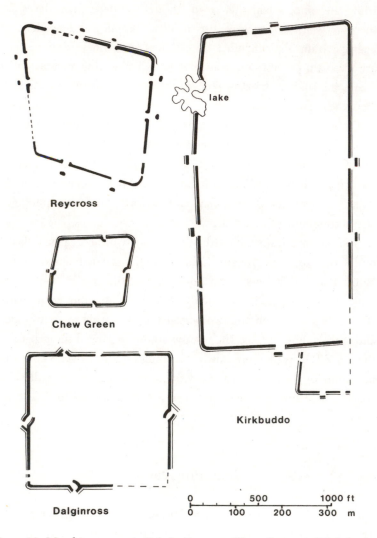

Figure 13 Marching camps in Britain. Reycross, Chew Green, and Dalginross date to the first century: the gates on the last camp are particularly significant. Kirkbuddo was probably erected during the Severan campaigns of the early third century.

suggest additional defenses in the form of caltrops or tree trunks with sharpened branches to impede an attack.

Wide entrances lay on each side of the camp, usually two on the longer side. These provided flexibility of movement for the soldiers but they were also weak points, so each was protected by a detached section of rampart and ditch or a curving section of rampart and ditch, which funneled would-be attackers in a particular direction.

We have two accounts of the layout of marching camps, Polybius writing in the second century BC and pseudo-Hyginus who used material from the middle years of the second century AD, that is 300 years later. There are differences between the two accounts, which is unsurprising in view of the gap in time between them. Pseudo-Hyginus provides useful details about the space allocations. A century of eighty men required a large tent for the centurion and eight tents each occupied by eight soldiers; the total was sixty-four because two tent groups of sixteen men were on duty at any one time. Space was left in front of each tent for the soldiers' armor and equipment. The allocation of space for one century was 120 by 30 Roman feet (about 35 × 9 meters).

Many have tried to relate the figures provided by Polybius and pseudo-Hyginus to surviving camps in an attempt to determine the size of the army that occupied them. There is, however, no agreement between archaeologists on the most appropriate equation. Rebecca Jones has suggested that the most generous figures for space allocation would allow 40,000 soldiers and a baggage train to occupy the largest known camp in Britain, St. Leonards in southern Scotland, which covers 70 hectares.

More camps survive in Britain than in any other part of the Empire. Some have been linked by size and structural details, with each group being assigned to a specific campaign. This allows us to suggest how far an army might march in a day. The camps in one line believed to date to the campaigns of Septimius Severus are about 11–15 kilometers apart; others are about 20 kilometers apart.

There is no doubt that the attention to detail, in camp building as well as all other aspects of military campaigning, served the Roman

army well. In his sixth season, the Roman governor of Britain, Julius
Agricola, divided his army into three groups. The camp holding the
Ninth Legion was attacked at night and its survival was partly the result
of its defenses. When reinforcements arrived, the enemy sought to
escape through the narrow camp gates and suffered heavy losses.

Exploration

The Roman army and fleet were used to explore the world around the
Empire. It has been suggested that in the case of Augustus several of his
expeditions were probes with a view to possible further expansion, as
much as campaigns to deal with problems with Rome's neighbors. Yet
these expeditions were trespassing into areas hitherto unexplored by
Rome's armies, and the accounts of their exploits are as informative
about the logistical problems as they are about the terrain.

Augustus sent an army up the Nile in 25 BC to deal with a frontier
problem caused by the actions of the kingdom of Ethiopia. The Roman
general, Petronius, did not stick to the Nile, but cut across the desert
at the Nile bend, which demonstrates that local knowledge was
available to him. Nero also sent an expedition up the Nile, this time
including part of the Praetorian Guard. In 61, they journeyed far south,
reaching the marshes beyond the junction of the White Nile and the
Sobat above Fashoda (now Kodok) where French and British armies
met in 1898.

In 25 BC, Augustus dispatched a fleet down the Red Sea. This was
partly military exploration and partly directed against the commercial
control of shipping by the Arabs. The expedition literally sailed into the
unknown. It progressed about a third of the way down the Red Sea
before pausing on the eastern side. Here, it experienced problems with
supplies and the soldiers suffered from bad food and a lack of water,
staying through the summer and winter to recover, before setting out
across the desert with camels carrying water. Eighty days brought the
expedition to a fertile area where it was able to replenish supplies.

Unfortunately, the army relied on local guides who misled it and eventually it turned back, arriving at the port of Myos Hormos on the west coast of the Red Sea, depleted in numbers as a result of disease, fatigue, and hunger. The story of this expedition reminds us of the self-confidence of the Romans—that they were prepared to launch an expedition into unknown territory, relying on allies and local guides, frequently coming unstuck.

Other Augustan expeditions in Africa brought Roman troops to Garama over 600 kilometers south of the Mediterranean coast of modern Libya in 19 BC, presumably utilizing the oases along the way. In 42, Suetonius Paulinus crossed the Atlas Mountains in North Africa in pursuit of Moors and crossed deserts of black dust, an area uninhabited because of the heat.

In northern climes, a Roman fleet reached the northernmost tip of Jutland in 5 AD, but other expeditions in the North Sea suffered in storms, Germanicus in 16 experiencing catastrophic losses when his 1000-strong fleet was caught in a gale. Agricola had more success when he sent his fleet to explore the northern reaches of Britain after his victory at the Battle of Mons Graupius in 83.

The Roman army was a multi-purpose—and adventurous—tool. But it could suffer from the disadvantage of operating in unknown lands, subject to extreme climatic conditions, open to the treachery of guides, and prey to problems of supply and strange food.

4

The Fighting Tactics of the Roman Army

*There should be silence until the enemy comes within weapon range,
and then everyone should utter a great war cry.*

Arrian, *Expedition against the Alans*, 25

Throughout its history, the Roman army fought three types of foes. Their more sophisticated enemies lay in North Africa where they fought the Carthaginians and the Numidians, and in the East where there were the Greek kingdoms and later the Parthians and their successors the Sassanids. Rome's European enemies, after Italy had been conquered, were not so well armed, well trained, and disciplined; they were certainly not professional armies, though they might be warlike in outlook. The final foe was another Roman army. There were civil wars not only in the last century of the Republic, but in 68–69, 193–197, from 235 to 284, and again intermittently during the fourth century.

Each type of warfare—as well as the battles—was different. A centralized Greek or North African kingdom would often capitulate after losing a single battle. In contrast, a strong and determined foe, such as the Dacians, could be resilient and it would take considerable effort to bring it to its knees. Throughout the rest of Europe, however, each tribe required to be conquered in turn and, as each tribe fielded not a professional army but rather the tribe-in-arms, it might rise up again after an initial defeat. This was certainly the experience of Caesar in Gaul. It is difficult to characterize the civil wars of Rome. Those of the late Republic were long-drawn out affairs, while that of 68–69 lasted a matter of months, though complicated by the actions which hostile elements took while Rome was preoccupied with its own affairs. Severus successfully seized the throne in the aftermath of the murder of Commodus on the last day of 192, but it took him nearly four years to defeat his rivals for power. Yet, one aspect is common to them all; they ranged widely across the Empire, from Britain to Judaea.

The soldier of the Roman imperial army was well trained for battle. In his account of the Roman army in *The Jewish War*, Josephus emphasized the training and discipline, backed up by planning and organization, which made it such a formidable fighting force. This army, unlike many of its enemies, could maneuver on the battlefield and was not fazed by having to fight a larger army. Of course, Rome did not win every battle, but it rarely lost a war. In view of the arrangements for choosing commanders for the army, whereby social status itself was regarded as the appropriate qualification, it is surprising that more battles were not lost. When necessary, however, the state was prepared to break the rules and appoint the best general for the job whether it was Scipio Africanus under the Republic or Claudius Pompeianus under Marcus.

The Roman army marched—and fought—in order. To maintain that order required discipline and training, which in turn brought confidence. Each soldier was allowed a space of about 1 meter by 2 meters to move, stand, and fight, the greater depth essential to allow him to throw his *pilum*. When drawn up for battle, the army might be arranged three, four, eight or more deep, depending on the circumstances and perhaps the tradition of that particular army. Only the first two lines made direct contact with the enemy. Their comrades behind them, however, not only took their place as the first ranks fell or tired, but also prevented them fleeing as well as intimidating the enemy by virtue of their very numbers. The centurion's deputy, the *optio*, stayed at the rear to maintain order and prevent soldiers from deserting. The legionaries were supported in battle by skirmishers operating in advance or on the wings, and perhaps archers behind. The legionaries advanced slowly into battle, and in silence, often in the face of a barrage of noise from their opponents. When nearing the enemy, they threw their javelins, issued their own shout and, at the signal from the trumpets, drew their swords and charged. At this point, in the face of the abrupt change from the slow silent advance to the noisy charge, the enemy sometimes broke and fled. Otherwise, the front rows fought each other, but not for long as it was strenuous work; comrades stepped in from behind and, where possible, pushed forward until the other side broke. At this point, casualties mounted, for the men fleeing could more easily be cut down from behind than in face-to-face combat. The cavalry completed the rout. That at least was how the battle ought to proceed from the Roman point-of-view.

Standards and trumpets

An important element in a battle—and in the life of the Roman soldier in general—was the legion's main standard, the eagle. This was the focus of the soldiers' loyalty and a potent symbol of the legion. To lose the eagle in battle, as happened to Crassus at Carrhae in 53 BC and Varus in Germany in AD 9, was considered a disgrace. Augustus was triumphant at achieving the return of Crassus' eagles and Germanicus reclaimed those lost by Varus. In a telling anecdote, Caesar's troops invading Britain in 55 BC were reluctant to land and were only persuaded by the eagle bearer of the Tenth Legion, who leapt ashore encouraging his comrades to follow rather than lose the eagle; his fellow soldiers, stung by the rebuke, followed him.

Each legion had other standards; one bore the symbol of the legion and the other the image of the emperor. Each century also had its own standard. In peacetime, the standards were housed in the temple in the regiment's headquarters building. But in war, each had a part to play.

The standards helped the soldiers line themselves up for battle and to move around the battlefield. Trumpets supplemented the standards. In an account of one of Caesar's battles, a trumpeter sounded the advance without orders and this was repeated so that all soldiers moved forward. On another occasion, however, it was the horn that sounded the charge. These instruments were also used for sounding instructions in the camp, for sleeping and rising as well as the watch.

One further standard deserves mention, the flag. This was not like a modern flag borne on a vertical pole, but one hanging from a crossbar, which itself was attached to a vertical pole. It was often used as a standard by detachments, bearing the name of the legion. It played a significant role in one battle—that of the Milvian Bridge fought just north of Rome in 312. Constantine placed the Christian symbol on his flag—and won the battle. This type of flag was adopted by the Christian church and now can be seen in many churches masquerading as the Mothers' Union banner. In the East, the image of the emperor on standards was replaced by the figure of Christ and that banner remains in use in the Orthodox Church.

Strategy

Roman generals developed different strategies for the various military situations they faced. Sometimes this was simply to march out and meet the enemy head-on. In the face of the enormous threat posed by Hannibal, Q. Fabius Maximus refused to give battle fearing that if he lost, Rome's allies would desert her; his successors gave battle, and lost. Cannae was one of Rome's greatest defeats. Some generals, notably Caesar, relied on speed, usually resulting in a surprise attack to help them achieve their aims. Sometimes the approach was simply to wear down the enemy by constant action, such as keeping an army in the field all year, or cutting off supplies so that the enemy starved. When the end came, the retribution meted out by Rome to those cities which did not surrender to her or to allies who deserted her was horrific; the cities were sacked, the inhabitants murdered or sold into slavery.

While the Romans could inflict what to us are hideous barbarities on their enemies, they still liked a justification to wage war. When recording Agricola's campaigns in Britain, Tacitus stated that in 82, the governor invaded Caledonia because he feared the threatening actions of his enemies. It is hard not to believe that this is a justification for the invasion rather than a response to a real threat; and even if the threat existed, it was the Romans who had invaded Caledonia the year before.

The Republican system of government did not encourage cooperation between consuls, but that was to change under the sole rule of Augustus. The Romans had used the pincer movement previously, such as against Hannibal, but now it could be employed more safely. Tiberius and his brother Drusus invaded Raetia in 15 BC, the former from the west and the latter from the south. Tiberius assembled two armies for his invasion of Bohemia in AD 4, each invading from a different direction.

There were still rivalries between generals during the Empire. In 54, Nero ordered his generals to invade Armenia. The plan was for Corbulo to attack from the north and his colleague, Paetus, from the west. Unfortunately, they did not get on and when Paetus was besieged, Corbulo moved so slowly to his rescue that Paetus was forced to surrender; Corbulo took over sole command. The last time we know of the use of the pincer movement was in 363 when Julian's army advanced on Ctesiphon. One column proceeded down the Euphrates and the other along the Tigris. The danger of his strategy was revealed when Julian reached his destination first and defeated the Persian army, but his other column was defeated. In the face of stronger numbers, Julian's army was forced to retreat, constantly harassed by the Persians and running out of supplies. In a skirmish, Julian was wounded and died that night; so ended the dynasty of Constantine the Great.

Battles against the Carthaginians and Parthians

We have already discussed some battles between the Romans and the Carthaginians, and seen how Scipio Africanus learnt to vary his battle line in the face of Hannibal's genius. Perhaps most notable was the Battle of Ilipa, fought in 206 BC against the Carthaginian general Hasdrubal Gisco, because it demonstrated the value of training in allowing him to maneuver his army on the battlefield. This was an important consideration, as battles did not always develop as the commanding officer anticipated.

In the Parthians, Rome faced a very different form of fighting. Their main strength lay in their cavalry. They had both light and heavy cavalry. The role of the former, whose men did not wear armor, was to harry the enemy with arrows; their fire power was such that they required an artillery train to keep them replenished. The light cavalry maintained its attack until the enemy was so weakened that it was time to send in the heavily armed cavalry.

The most famous battle between the Romans and the Parthians was Carrhae, fought in 53 BC. M. Licinius Crassus set out from Syria with an army of nearly 50,000 men and marched across the desert, deliberately choosing the more direct though more dangerous route. He was harried by the Parthian general Surena, who commanded a smaller force, and whose task was to slow the progress of the Roman invasion. When the two armies met, Crassus was not only indecisive but he ignored the advice of his experienced officers. The Roman army was formed into a square and held out in the face of the arrows of the light-armed cavalry. A Roman cavalry force sent to disperse the Parthian artillery train was slaughtered, with Crassus' son committing suicide as a result of his defeat. This broke the morale of the Romans who withdrew. This offered the Parthians a heaven-sent opportunity, for it was easy to cut down stragglers. About 20,000 Roman soldiers were killed and 10,000 captured, and to add to the ignominy the eagles fell into Parthian hands. Thereafter, sensible Roman rulers sought to maintain peace with Parthia; others seeking glory thought otherwise, but nearly always to their cost. At Carrhae in 53 BC, the Romans suffered a massive defeat, but this was caused by a loss of nerve. The battle is important in underlining the importance of psychology in warfare.

The mobility of the Parthians was their most powerful weapon. Not only were they able to inflict pain on an advancing or retreating army, but also move swiftly to attack a detached column. In 37 BC, for example, Mark Antony lost his barrage train and two legions to a Parthian counterattack. Yet, the Parthians were not invincible and several Roman forces penetrated their kingdom, sacking their capital Ctesiphon in 117, 165, and 197. Parthian invasions of the Roman Empire tended to be hampered by their lack of siege equipment.

Romans versus Romans

The battle of Pharsalus in 48 BC is unusual in our records because we have two accounts of the action. One was by Caesar, the commander of the victorious army, and the other by Lucan, an aristocratic poet, writing in the reign of Nero—that is, about a hundred years after the battle. Both had axes to grind. Caesar wanted to show himself in the best light; Lucan, if not in the worst, certainly sought to depict him in a more unfavorable manner, not least because he was the ancestor of the despised Nero. Lucan, however, was cavalier with his facts, contradicting himself from time to time. Yet, the two accounts are generally similar, differing only in detail and emphasis.

Both accounts are useful because we can see how two Roman commanders faced up to one another. Pompey prepared his battle line with himself commanding two legions on the left flank, with a further two more in the center and a legion and some cohorts on the right wing. His less reliable troops were placed between the center and the two wings. To the left of his army were archers, slingers, and cavalry, his right flank being protected by a stream. Caesar followed a similar basic battle line, carefully locating his four legions, with himself to the right facing Pompey. Here he could observe the location of the enemy cavalry and, fearing being outflanked, he quickly withdrew one cohort from each legion's third line and created a fourth line against the cavalry threat. In this case, the battle developed as Caesar expected and he was able to use his reserve to attack Pompey's cavalry in the rear.

Caesar ordered his army not to move until he gave the command to advance with his flag. Upon the signal being given, Crastinus, formerly chief centurion of the Tenth Legion, charged the enemy, taking about 120 volunteers with him. In Lucan's account, however, Crastinus threw his javelin *before* the command, which was then given by the cornet and the trumpet. Caesar, it might be suspected, would prefer to gloss over this act of disobedience.

Pompey's army was on the higher ground; however, it did not charge downhill but waited for Caesar's army to tire itself by running uphill. Perceiving the tactic, however, they stopped about half way up, recovered, threw their javelins, drew their swords and charged. The soldiers of the Pompeian army maintained their order in the face of the flight of javelins, threw theirs and drew their swords. Pompey's cavalry attacked Caesar's flank but in turn were attacked from behind by Caesar's fourth line and as the cavalry retreated, Caesar's right wing moved forward and pushed Pompey's left wing back. At that point, Caesar ordered his third line forward; they took over from the tired first and second lines, forcing the Pompeians back until they broke and fled. The victory was achieved through Caesar correctly reading how the battle would develop together with his use of a well-trained and experienced army.

The value of commanding such an army was shown at Philippi in 42. Although not all Antony's maneuvers worked, he demonstrated that he was more inventive than his opponents and eventually won the contest. Augustus was altogether different. He did not cover himself in glory at Philippi, losing his camp, but one interpretation of later events is that he realized his deficiencies and thereafter entrusted the generalship to others, in particular Agrippa, while concentrating on the wider strategic issues.

Few detailed descriptions of the battles of Rome's later civil wars survive. An interesting example is the Battle of Turin in 312 between the armies of the rival emperors Constantine and Maxentius. To counteract the force of Maxentius' heavy cavalry, Constantine spread his battle line so that the cavalry charged through it into the midst of his army. Here Constantine's light cavalry, armed with metal-tipped clubs, attacked Maxentius' cavalry. His infantry then attacked and broke Maxentius' infantry who were slaughtered before the city walls. Constantine's tactics reflected those of Scipio Africanus at Zama.

Romans in Europe

It would be easy to suggest that the Romans had many advantages over their "barbarian" opponents and therefore assume that they would always win. This, however, was not the case. One of the most famous Roman defeats was the Battle of the Teutoberg Forest in AD 9, in which three legions and several auxiliary regiments were destroyed.

The Battle of the Teutoberg Forest

Germany between the rivers Rhine and Elbe had been under Roman rule for a generation when P. Quinctilius Varus was appointed governor. He was an experienced administrator and soldier—he had quashed a rebellion in Judaea some years earlier—and was a member of the imperial family having married, successively, two great-nieces of Augustus. In AD 9, he was leading his army of three legions and auxiliaries, perhaps 18–20,000 strong, back to winter quarters when it was ambushed in the forest. Varus committed several errors: he had weakened his army by placing some soldiers on garrison duty; he ignored advice, or at least hints, from his German allies, that all was not well; he did not send out advance patrols; he did not march in approved order but allowed the camp followers to become mixed up with the soldiers; and he allowed his column to stretch for up to 20 kilometers— in short, he had relaxed his guard. On the other hand, he was not to know that one of his German allies, Arminius, was leading him into a trap, and it was not his fault that there was a storm, making the ground muddy. Arminius deserted and his men attacked the Roman column. In spite of that, the Romans managed to create a camp for the night. The next morning they broke out, but lost many men in the attempt. In the continuing rain, their shields became heavy and their bow-strings useless. They walked into another trap and were slaughtered. Varus committed suicide.

As a result of excavations that began in 1988, the site of the battle was identified at Kalkriese near Osnabruck. Fragments of Roman armor and weapons were found together with a wide range of other artifacts and coins over a stretch of ground 24 kilometers long and about a kilometer wide. It would appear that a bank of earth had been constructed by the Germans to impede the progress of the Romans or funnel them in a particular direction.

A younger Augustus would have bounced back but the emperor was now in his seventies and merely consolidated the military defense on the Rhine. Five years later, Germanicus invaded Germany. He campaigned there for three seasons. He, too, was ambushed but escaped. And he also suffered from the weather when his fleet was damaged by storms in the North Sea. After three seasons, Tiberius judged that the cost was too great—in one telling anecdote, it was remarked that Germanicus had used up all the horses in Gaul for his campaigns—and brought the campaigning to a halt; Germany was too great for the Romans to absorb.

Battles in Britain

Tacitus and Dio describe several battles in Britain, but in these cases the Romans won. In 49, the new governor, Ostorius Scapula, was faced with an enemy attack on Rome's allies. He dealt with this expeditiously and then disarmed tribes whose loyalty was suspect. This in turn led to an uprising by one of these tribes, the Iceni. It was they who chose the site of the battle and, no doubt appreciating the strength of the Roman army, they sought extra protection by choosing a site with a narrow approach and further protected this by constructing a rampart. This availed them naught, however. The Romans undertook a frontal attack, trapping the Britons with their own rampart.

In the final British battle against Caratacus, the Britons again protected themselves with a rampart. In this instance, they were on the higher ground and the rampart was built in the dips; in front flowed a river, which was not easy to cross. After careful reconnoitering, Ostorius chose a crossing point over the river and attacked the rampart with his men protected by means of the tortoise formation (Figure 14). The

Figure 14 The "tortoise" formation. Roman legionaries advance toward a Dacian stronghold under the protection of their shields.

fighting was evenly matched for a time, but the Roman strength ensured victory, aided, stated Tacitus, by the Britons' lack of body armor and helmets.

The conquest of Britain included a naval engagement. Suetonius Paulinus, an experienced general, transported his army across the Menai Straits in flat-bottomed boats with the cavalry fording the channel or swimming. The aim was to destroy a stronghold of the Druids. On the shoreline, the Roman soldiers were met by armed men, women brandishing torches, and druids uttering curses, which momentarily unnerved them, but they swept on to victory—and destroyed the sacred groves.

While Paulinus was in Anglesey, rebellion broke out to his rear led by Boudica, queen of the Iceni. The Roman response was normal. A rapid task force attempted to squash the rebellion but, in this case, failed, apparently with the loss of a considerable part of a legion. Paulinus gathered the remainder of the army together and with a much more powerful force marched against Boudica. On this occasion, it was the Roman commander who chose a narrow defile, as this would prevent him being surrounded by the much larger British force—Dio stated that the British army numbered 230,000. The Roman army was placed at the mouth of the defile with open land beyond. The legionaries were drawn up in close ranks with the auxiliary infantry on each side and the cavalry beyond; Dio stated that Paulinus divided his army into three groups, and Tacitus' description would support that. As the armies drew closer, the Britons sang battle songs and shouted while the Romans moved silently forward until they came close enough to throw their javelins. They then charged—Tacitus says in a wedge formation—while the Britons were still walking and broke through the ranks of their enemies. Dio describes a scene in which cavalry charged cavalry, Roman archers fired on enemy chariots, but sometimes had to give way. The Romans had to close their ranks against the chariots, but in other places were scattered by them. Such fights went on in all three divisions before the Romans prevailed. The Britons fled, their flight hampered by their carts. According to Tacitus, 80,000 Britons perished, including women, but only 400 Romans.

In the final battle described by Tacitus, Mons Graupius, the enemy again used a hillside to help strengthen its position. He stated that when Agricola arrived at the site, he found the Graupian Mountain occupied by over 30,000 Caledonians and their allies led by Calgacus. It is not easy to know the strength of the Roman army in spite of several figures being given. Agricola placed his 8,000 auxiliaries in the center of his battle line with the 3,000 cavalry on the flanks (Figure 15). The legions were stationed behind, in front of the camp. Although Agricola could draw on the soldiers from four legions, a strong detachment from Britain was serving in Germany at the time, so his army was seriously depleted.

The battle started with a display by the enemy chariots on the plain in front of the Roman army. Now, stated Tacitus, Agricola, fearing the

Figure 15 An auxiliary soldier fighting. The soldier uses his shield as a weapon; his spear was in metal and has been subsequently removed from the Column.

enemy's superior numbers, extended his battle line by opening up his ranks. The Romans threw their javelins; the Britons responded with their spears. Agricola then ordered the auxiliary regiments to close with the enemy. Here Tacitus contrasted the superior weapons of the Romans, their stabbing swords and heavy shields, which could themselves be used as weapons, with those of the Caledonians' enormous slashing swords with no points and their small shields. The cohorts pressed forward across the plain and up the slopes. The Britons higher up the hill moved down to outflank the Romans, so Agricola sent in the four regiments of his reserve cavalry, about 2,000 men. This turned the battle. The cavalry swung round and attacked the Caledonians from the rear and the enemy broke and fled (Figure 16). For a time they regrouped in a wood, but they were flushed out. Ten thousand Britons were killed with the loss of just 360 Romans, including the commander of a cohort.

Figure 16 A cavalryman rides down his enemies. This scene on the Bridgeness distance slab on the Antonine Wall is an iconic image of a Roman cavalryman in action riding down his foes, who cower on the ground under the hooves of his horse.

Two of the recurring themes of the battles in Britain were the enemy's use of higher ground to their advantage and rivers to protect themselves. The latter occurs twice during the initial campaign of 43, and again in the battle against Caratacus; the invasion of Anglesey was a rather different situation. Such protection did not help, not least because the Romans were trained to cross rivers, including one as wide as the

Danube. Nor did the guerrilla tactics employed by the Britons achieve success. Dio describes these graphically in relation to the campaigns of Septimius Severus in Scotland in 209 and 210. The enemy put out sheep and cattle, which the Roman soldiers went to seize and were lured on until they were worn out. When the army became dispersed, individual soldiers were picked on and when injured were killed by their own comrades to prevent them falling into enemy hands. As a result, no pitched battles were fought but the Romans are said to have lost 50,000 men—surely an exaggeration, not least in view of the calculations of the numbers, which could be quartered in the large camps that we believe were used during this campaign. Nevertheless, Severus pressed forward, almost to the end of the island, and the Caledonians were forced to sue for peace. On no occasion did guerrilla tactics work: the Romans simply replied with devastation that eventually led the enemy to negotiate.

The Battle of Strasbourg

In the middle of the fourth century, Julian met another foreign army, on this occasion the Alamanni at the Battle of Strasbourg fought in 357 on the Rhine frontier. The Alamanni had defeated the Romans before and were confident of victory, as they outnumbered the Romans by more than 2:1. Julian recalled his outposts (unlike Varus) and, at the call of the trumpets, his army advanced in silence behind the standards. When closer to the enemy, Julian gave the usual speech and one of the standard-bearers urged the men on. In his account of the battle, Ammianus Marcellinus describes how each side weighed up the disposition of the other and located their troops accordingly. The Romans placed their cavalry (which included heavy cavalry and archers) on the right flank, so the Alamanni followed suit. On their right flank, the Alamanni hid men ready to ambush the Roman advance.

The legions were drawn up in two main lines, with additional troops on the flanks. Trumpeters from both sides sounded the start of the battle. The Alamanni charged first and broke the Roman cavalry, who retreated behind the legions where they regrouped and rejoined the battle. The

Alamanni charged again and broke the Roman infantry's front line, but failed to break the second line and were forced back until they turned and fled. Roman losses were light, just 247, against 6,000 Alamanni dead with many more perishing as they tried to cross the Rhine, and they suffered the ultimate indignity of their king being captured.

The account of the battle was by Ammianus Marcellinus and his description could almost be of any battle during the Roman Empire. His details are telling: the use of the trumpets and the standards; the silence of the Romans; the evenness of the fight when engaged at close quarters; the strength of the Alamanni balanced by the discipline of the Romans; and, most importantly for the narrator, the coolness, courage, and strategic sense of his hero, Julian.

The Battle of Adrianople

Twenty years later, a Roman defeat was to have far-reaching consequences. The Battle of Adrianople was fought in 378, but its causes tell us something about the decline of the Roman Empire (Adrianople is modern Edirne in Turkish Thrace). Two years before, Goths had sought and had been granted permission to settle within the Empire. There was land where they could live, presumably because of a decline in population. Local friction, mainly caused by corrupt Roman officials, led to an uprising of the Goths. The Emperor Valens came in person to deal with the situation, seeking military glory.

Valens pitched camp outside the city of Adrianople and held a Council of War. Opinion was divided but the emperor declined to wait for the arrival of his brother's army from the west and gave battle. After marching for seven hours, he drew up his forces facing the Goths who stood in front of a hill on which a circle of wagons protected their civilians. Negotiations started but over-eager Roman soldiers attacked the Goths. They were repulsed and the Roman cavalry attack on the left wing, which had reached the wagons, failed through lack of support. The Gothic cavalry swept down on the Roman army, which was too tightly packed to maneuver or fight effectively—Ammianus stated that the soldiers did not have space to draw their swords—while visibility was obscured by dust through which arrows rained down on the Roman army (Vegetius emphasized the danger of dust in a battle). The Romans fought fiercely but were overwhelmed by superior numbers and broke. In flight, they were cut down. In the melee, the emperor, several generals, and many officers were killed. Ammianus likened the defeat to Cannae, though about a third of the Roman army escaped.

How the great military tradition of Rome had fallen. Over-confidence, ill-discipline, a lack of care for the comfort and welfare of its soldiers, an absence of forethought in preparing for battle, each of these had contributed. Yet some aspects were little different from earlier times, the failure of military leadership in particular. But whereas six centuries before Rome had been able to raise a new army, it was now more difficult in the declining decades of the Empire.

Naval battles

We have already seen that the Romans created a naval force before their wars with Carthage. However, in these wars, faced with the superior naval experience of the Carthaginians, the Romans invented a new fighting weapon, a boarding plank, virtually turning a battle between ships into a land battle on ships.

The most famous naval battle was at Actium, where Augustus defeated Mark Antony. Augustus had a fleet of about 400 ships, but Antony was only able to crew some 230–240 warships, burning the rest; the reserve commanded by Cleopatra was sixty ships strong. Each fleet tried to outflank the other and in time a gap opened in Antony's fleet. At that point, Cleopatra, instead of moving to fill the gap, turned and sailed for Egypt. Antony's fleet disintegrated and he followed the queen with but a few ships.

While Rome controlled the Mediterranean, there were few naval battles, but in 324 an engagement took place in the Hellespont between the fleets of Constantine, commanded by his son Crispus, and the rival emperor Licinius. Crispus advanced into the narrow strait with eighty vessels, his small force encouraging Licinius' admiral Amandus to employ over twice that number. But his 200 ships had no room to maneuver, which gave the advantage to Crispus. His victory was secured by a favorable wind on the second day of the engagement. Amandus lost 120 ships, mostly by being driven onto the rocks, and fled the battle.

Siege warfare

The sieges of Numantia by Scipio Aemilianus in 133 BC and of Alesia by Julius Caesar in 52 BC have already been described (pp. 24–5). Caesar also adopted siege tactics against Pompey at Dyrrhachium in 48 BC. Perhaps the most famous siege works, however, are those associated with the Jewish War fought by Vespasian and his son Titus from 66 to 73.

The war involved battles and the harrying of the local population, but is chiefly remembered for its sieges, including Jotapata, Jerusalem, Machaerus, and Masada. In each case, the Romans surrounded the city with camps and a circumvallation and created a large mound to provide access to the city walls they were attacking. At Jotapata, they used both bolt-firing machines and stone-throwing machines, especially to clear the city walls of defenders while the mound was being built. The walls were then attacked with a battering ram, the soldiers protecting themselves by the tortoise formation (Figure 14). The defenders sought to counter the blows of the ram by lowering bags of chaff while also heightening the walls, but this did not prevent the walls being breached. At that point, Vespasian ordered attacks all around the city to reduce the number of men defending the breach.

At Jerusalem, the siege was complicated by the size of the city as well as its defenses. Each wall had to be broken through, and each was well defended by the Jews who led several counterattacks. Although the Romans gained entry to the city, and destroyed many houses in order to give themselves room for maneuver, they were still faced by a second wall and then by the citadel containing the Temple. Siege ramps were constructed and destroyed twice, the second time by undermining, before the Temple compound was captured after several weeks of fighting. Finally, the remainder of the city was captured. From start to finish, the siege lasted four months.

The last Jewish stronghold to hold out was Masada, situated on a rocky eminence 400 meters high. The Romans surrounded it with a stone wall equipped with towers while eight camps housed their troops. A ramp was constructed on one side for the siege engines but before the final thrust, the Jewish defenders committed mass suicide.

The Romans won their sieges by a combination of overwhelming force and perseverance. They doggedly stuck to the task and could afford to take their time while the inhabitants of each city slowly starved.

There were occasions when the Romans were themselves besieged. During Caesar's Gallic War, the winter quarters of one of his generals, Cicero, brother of the famous orator, was attacked. During the first night of the siege, the soldiers fortified the camp with towers as well as repairing the ramparts. After daily attacks, the Romans had to repair their damaged defenses at night as well as getting themselves ready for the next day's assault. The towers were raised even higher and more spears were made. The attackers created their own circumvallation and sought to fill in the Roman ditches. Fire arrows set light to the wooden huts within the camp and all the soldiers' possessions were destroyed. The siege was eventually lifted by the arrival of Caesar himself.

Another account of a siege is that of Ammianus Marcellinus, who was a staff officer in the city of Amida when attacked by the Persians in 359. The repeated Persian attacks were unsuccessful, though the defenders were gradually weakened by disease. A local citizen revealed a secret entrance to the city and the Persians captured a tower but were driven out. A Roman foray into the Persian camp was in turn repulsed. The siege ended when the Roman attempt to strengthen the walls resulted in the collapse of a section of it, and the Persians entered the city. Ammianus managed to escape to write his first-hand account of life on the frontiers of Rome.

Excavations at Dura-Europos on the Euphrates have provided archaeological evidence for a siege. In 256, the city was besieged by the

Sassanid king Shapur I. His troops dug a mine below one of the towers and when the Romans discovered this, they excavated a counter-mine. Soldiers of the two armies met underground; when Roman soldiers fleeing from the countermine suggested to the defenders that the Sassanians would appear next, they sealed the countermine even though some Romans remained within it, where they died. The action, however, caused the Sassanians to abandon their mine. The Sassanians made another attempt at mining but eventually created a ramp and stormed the city from that. Evidence shows that the Sassanians used poisonous gases, created by burning bitumen and sulphur, in the mines. In an earlier siege at Marseille, the defenders flooded the mines, which led to their collapse.

Sieges required special equipment. The army made the towers and the sheds to protect their battering rams on site. During the attack, they used catapults, which fired stones or iron bolts. These were relatively small and could be mounted on top of a siege tower. Of an altogether different scale was the one-armed *ballista*, known as the *onager*, wild ass, which fired a single large stone. It had been invented by the Greeks, like so much of the artillery perfected by the Romans, and was described by Trajan's architect Apollodorus and also by Ammianus 150 years later. Eight men were required to wind back the arm and in a particularly lurid anecdote, Ammianus described an accident in which the machine misfired and the engineer in charge of the *onager* was hit and his body so smashed that not all the pieces could be found.

Artillery formed part of the equipment of a legion, and later auxiliary units. According to Vegetius, each legionary cohort had one *onager*, and each century a catapult drawn by mules with eleven soldiers to operate it. The catapults were used in battle as well as sieges. Arrian, when about to do battle with the Alani in 134, placed his catapults on the flanks where they gained an advantage from the higher ground. From here they took part in the opening salvo.

There is a strong possibility that the camps on each side of the late prehistoric hill-fort at Burnswark in south-west Scotland were part of a training ground for soldiers of the Roman army in Britain.

5

The Peacetime Army

Their exercises are bloodless battles and their battles are bloody exercises.

Josephus, *The Jewish War*, 3, 5, 1

There were three main duties for the soldiers of the Roman army: defending the Empire, controlling its inhabitants, and protecting the person of the emperor. During the Republic, new lands had been conquered by the legions (or given to Rome), but this became less common under the Empire. Now, the extent of the Empire was determined by the emperor himself, as Domitius Corbulo was to note when he was pulled back from military action north of the Rhine in 47; lucky were the Roman generals of old, he remarked. The legions and auxiliary units were still called upon to conquer new territory at times— Britain under Claudius, Dacia and Parthia under Trajan, for example— but increasingly their role became one of defending what the Romans already possessed. Sometimes this involved major warfare. In 86, for example, the provincial governor of Moesia and the praetorian prefect were both killed during invasions across the Danube by the Dacians. But for the most part, the army was not involved in dealing with major invasions, but rather frontier control. Forts were spread out along the frontier lines, and soldiers sought to prevent raiding and enforce the regulations that governed passage through these frontiers.

Over the years, particular areas became more pacified and no longer needed military surveillance, while new pressure points developed along the frontiers and units were moved to deal with them. Under Augustus and his immediate successors, many legions were based on the Rhine located so as to invade Germany when the order was given, but, after the abortive campaigns of Germanicus, it never came. As it became clear that the greater threat came from the kingdom of the Dacians in modern Transylvania, several legions were moved to the Lower Danube to protect the eastern provinces. But the process slowed so that full legions stopped being moved in the later second century and only detachments were transferred to the battle zone. In these circumstances, units settled down in one spot and sometimes stayed there for centuries.

The army may have put down roots, but training continued. Thorough training was one of the secrets of the success of the Roman army. But before any training, recruits had to be selected. We have already seen the procedures adopted by the Republic when the army was the citizen body in arms. Under the Empire, matters were different. Crucially, the army was a volunteer force with the levy only resorted to in times of crisis.

Recruitment

Throughout the first three centuries of the Empire, the Roman army relied mainly on voluntary recruitment. Conscription was only resorted to in time of need, such as after the Varian Disaster of AD 9. In the time of Augustus and Tiberius, the legions serving in the western provinces were primarily recruited from Italy, but the percentage of Italians fell until by the time of Hadrian there were hardly any, although it would appear that new legions continued to be raised in Italy throughout the second century while Italians served in the units based in Rome. Instead, their places in the legions were taken by men from Provence (southern France), Spain and Africa, and from the second century by men from the frontier provinces. In the east, local recruitment was also normal but there were fewer Roman citizens, so recruits might be given citizenship on enlistment. The auxiliary regiments were drawn from the frontier tribes and states and this continued to be the general pattern.

There appears to have been a clear trend: the longer an area was part of the Empire, the less likely its inhabitants were to join the army. There were two results. In the fourth century, military service became enforced, with recruits provided by cities and landowners, or hereditary, and greater recourse was made to the recruitment of peoples from beyond the Empire. Perhaps nothing exemplifies this more than the account of the elevation of Constantine to be emperor at York in 306. His main supporter was Crocus, king of the Alamanni, a people who had ravaged the German frontiers of the Empire throughout the third century.

Potential recruits had to present themselves for interview at what we would call a recruiting office. Vegetius emphasized that it was essential to choose recruits with care. Each potential recruit passed through two initial stages: an examination of his qualifications followed by an examination of his fighting abilities. Vegetius recommended that recruits should be countrymen as they were more used to hard work, and they should be from more manly trades—smiths, carpenters, butchers, and huntsmen would therefore make good recruits. Interestingly, Vegetius stated that the recruiting officer should also look for quickness of mind and also a good education, as the ability to read and write was important for the organization of the army.

The was a basic height qualification of 1.67 meters but those wishing to join the Praetorian Guard, the first cohort of a legion or a cavalry unit, the requirement was six Roman feet (1.7 meters), though these criteria could be relaxed in certain circumstances. Vegetius described the perfect recruit: he should have a lively eye and carry his head erect, his chest should be broad, his shoulders muscular, his arms strong, and so on. Analysis of inscriptions indicates that most men joined the army between the ages of eighteen and twenty-three, though recruits as young as thirteen and as old as thirty-six are recorded.

The recruit also had to be free born, that is not a freedman or a slave. Pliny's letters demonstrate that the punishment for a slave who had tried to enlist by not declaring his status was death. Freedmen (former slaves) might be enlisted in an emergency but they were organized into special units. Those men who wished to join the legions had not only to be free born but also Roman citizens. A junior officer in a legion in Egypt in 92 appears to have had doubt cast on his status, for he produced an affidavit confirming that he was of free birth and a Roman citizen and this was supported by the oaths of three comrades.

There were other restrictions on joining the army. Men who had been condemned to death, deported to an island, exiled for a fixed term but had escaped, tried for a capital offence, convicted for adultery or another major crime were not eligible for military service. At the end of the fourth century, a decree stipulated that slaves, men from inns or houses of ill repute, cooks and bakers were debarred from military service. It is clear that it was a serious crime for such men to seek to join the army.

The Roman world thrived on letters of recommendation, as the letters of the Younger Pliny demonstrate. Such recommendations were important both for would-be recruits as well as those subsequently seeking promotion. Claudius Terentianus wrote to his father mentioning such letters, and he also said that he had failed to join a legion because of a poor reference, so he enlisted in the fleet instead.

If the potential recruit was successful at this stage, he underwent a test of his physical abilities to determine whether he was capable of undergoing the training necessary to be a good soldier and whether he had sufficient courage and mental qualities. Some men were rejected at this stage.

At an early point in the process of recruitment, a file was opened on the potential soldier. Among the details recorded were his name, age, whether he had any distinguishing marks of identification, and the date he was registered on the rolls of the unit. The final actions in this recruitment process were the placing of an indelible mark on the skin, entry into the records, and the taking of an oath, which, with his colleagues, he would repeat twice a year for the length of his service. The trial of a man in 295 refers to a piece of lead round his neck, so perhaps soldiers also carried a particular form of identification.

Pay

Recruits were given three gold pieces.(*aurei*)—that is, 75 *denarii*—on enlistment. This was called "travel money", to pay for the soldier to travel to his regiment, but it was presumably also an inducement to join the army. This sum is recorded for soldiers joining auxiliary units and the fleet; as legionaries were paid in amounts of 75 *denarii*, it is probable that recruits to a legion received the same amount. The soldiers themselves, however, appear to have counted their money in a different way because Tacitus stated that one of the mutineers in 14 remarked that the legionaries were paid 10 *asses* a day and they wanted a pay raise to one *denarius* a day—that, is 16 *asses*, quite a demand! The use of *asses* to pay soldiers is supported by the discovery of several unworn coins of this denomination dating to 86 in some first-century Scottish forts. The best interpretation is that they are part of a supply of new coins sent to Britain to pay soldiers.

Thereafter, soldiers were paid three times a year. This appears to have occurred each time at a parade; Titus broke off the siege of Jerusalem in 70 not only to parade and pay his troops but also to bolster their confidence. Caesar doubled the pay of the legionaries to 225 *denarii* a year and Domitian increased it to 300 *denarii*, presumably by adding a fourth pay-day. Severus, and then his son Caracalla, increased pay further. The auxiliaries were paid less than the legionaries, with cavalry always receiving more than infantry.

In Republican times, a general would often share the booty won during campaigning with his soldiers. As such remunerative warfare became less common in the Empire, the use of a payment known as a donative was extended. These marked special occasions such as the accession of the emperor, an imperial marriage or a victory. Donatives could be very large. Augustus left every soldier 75 *denarii* or more in his will. Claudius gave each praetorian the equivalent of five years' pay on his accession. In the second century, such sums so depleted the Treasury that Marcus Aurelius had to sell off the palace furniture and his wife's clothes in order to recoup the money paid to the soldiers.

Soldiers might also make their own claims. The army of Vespasian sought "nail-money" to compensate for the damage to their boots in their long march to Rome in 69; the emperor told them to march bare-foot.

Each recruit had an account opened in his name in the camp bank (these accounts were kept by the standard-bearers of the centuries, though why we do not know). His "travel money" was paid into that account—the centurions of the First Cohort of Lusitanians based in Egypt in 117 recorded the deposit of the money of new recruits—and thereafter his pay. Soldiers had money deducted from their pay for various living expenses. The deductions included food, boots and straps, hay and the regimental Saturnalia, and the celebration of a religious festival that took place on December 17 (the recruit also had to be equipped; this is discussed in Chapter 6). The accounts of two soldiers serving in Egypt in 81 are in a form familiar to anyone preparing a balance sheet today, and, interestingly, are in different hands. The document records the first salary installment, followed by the deductions, and the remaining total; then follows the next installment, and so on. By the end of the year, the balance had risen from 201.5 drachmas to 343 drachmas. It seems that the money was retained in the unit's strong room in hard cash. On pay-day on January 1, 89, a rebellion was raised by L. Antonius Saturninus, governor of Upper Germany, and funded by the deposits of the two legions brigaded together at Mainz. This had at least two results: Domitian broke up double-legionary bases and restricted the depositing of more than 250 *denarii* by any one soldier (it is possible that this was also the occasion of the move of the pay-day), and the annual taking of the oath to the Roman state—from January 1 to January 3.

Joining the Roman army brought certain benefits, in addition to regular pay and food. This included the ability to make a military will (normally only Roman citizens could make a will). Soldiers were given special license to leave their possessions to their children, which was a necessary action, as they were not allowed to marry according to Roman law until about 200 but still might have children.

Training

Vegetius and other writers describe the training of soldiers. For recruits, this covered all aspects: the use of weapons morning and afternoon, drill and movements, the digging of ditches, the construction of palisades, running and jumping, swimming, vaulting onto a wooden horse, felling trees, and route marches four times a month. The army's instructors specialized in different activities such as drill and weaponry. Recruits were taught the two army paces, the short military pace and the longer full pace so that they could undertake the normal daily march of 30 kilometers, which should be completed in five hours. In this basic training, soldiers used special wooden practice swords, shields, spears and helmets, and used a wooden post to represent the enemy. The training was undertaken on the parade ground. It is possible that the halls that have been found in some forts were erected to allow training to continue under cover in inclement weather. Recruits were also taught the military rules, including not deserting their post and the need to maintain order in the ranks.

A secondy level of training was undertaken in the field. This included building practice camps, erecting tents and sleeping in them, and building roads—two milestones in Cyrenaica record the construction of a road by recruits.

This period of basic training lasted a minimum of four months, after which recruits were enrolled in a unit. In 103, the Prefect of Egypt wrote to the commanding officer of one of his units stating that he had approved six recruits and that they should be entered on the records with effect from February 19. The names of the soldiers are given, their ages (all between 20 and 25), and any distinguishing marks, such as "scar on left eyebrow", or "scar on left hand". The final entry in the letter is by the adjutant of the unit who recorded that the original letter was retained in the office of the cohort. Similar information was recorded in the documents of the Twentieth Cohort of Palmyrenes based at Dura on the Euphrates in the 230s. Two other letters interestingly state that soldiers might change their name when they joined the army. Once the recruit was formally enrolled in a unit, he would begin to be paid. This would, however, not be the end of his training, which, in theory at least, would continue throughout his military career.

Record-keeping

The recruit was now a member of a very large organization and within that body he had his own file, which recorded not only details of his service but also reports on his character and health, as well as his duties.

For soldiers on duty, the day at base started with a parade and roll call, which was also committed to paper. Fragments of several such reports relating to the Twentieth Cohort of Palmyrenes survive, one covering the four days from March 27 to March 30 in about 233. The report for each day started with the total number of men in the unit, which was then broken down into officers, camel riders, and cavalry. The password for the day was given next: Mercury on March 27, Security on another document. Then followed details of the soldiers sent elsewhere on specific duties, and those who had returned from such duties, as well as other significant information, such as new recruits or the arrival of letters from the governor. The orders for the day were announced, the oath taken—the soldiers swore "we will perform what has been ordered and are ready for all orders"—and the names of soldiers on watch at the standards specified. This daily report was usually about eight to ten lines long, so during the course of a year a substantial document would have been created.

Each year another report was prepared by each unit in the army, a return which it is believed went to Rome. These recorded the name of the regiment, the number of officers and men, additions and losses during the year, how many were ill (conjunctivitis was a common complaint), and how many soldiers were away from base and where. Their duties might include collecting clothing, food or horses (who also had their own files, incidentally), escort duty, guarding the mines or at an outpost. A final balance was provided at the end of the document.

In order that each soldier knew his duties, a timetable was prepared listing down the side the names of soldiers and across the top the days of the month: one such document exists for the Third Cyrenaican Legion in Egypt for part of the month of October in 87. A complete roster of all the men in each unit was also kept. Two near complete lists survive for the Twentieth Cohort of Palmyrenes for the years 219 and 222. They record the name of every man together with his rank, duty, status, and posting. It can therefore be seen that in both years, some soldiers were outposted at considerable distance from their main base.

The Roman army seems to have thrived on paperwork. There appears to have been a document for every action. An enigmatic list found at Vindolanda is for chickens and geese used in the commanding officer's house over a period of at least two years at the very beginning of the second century, but it does not state whether they were to be eaten or sacrificed.

Many of the records deal with supplies and the distribution of food. One list at Vindolanda is of the distribution of wheat from a barrel. It included not only the men to whom the wheat was given but sometimes their jobs—the oxherds at the wood, Amabilis at the shrine, Lucco in charge of the pigs—and also the amounts, ranging from 2 to 26 *modii*. A *modius* was equivalent to 16 *sextarii*. The Carvoran Modius, a bronze dry-measure found at the fort of Carvoran on Hadrian's Wall, states that it holds 17½ *sextarii* and it has been suggested that this is the supply of grain for a soldier for a week, the daily ration being 2½ *sextarii*. This is close to the ration recorded by Polybius, though he was using Greek measurements. These figures give us a weekly ration of just over one *modius*.

The lists found at Vindolanda are fascinating, if also frustrating because they are fragmentary. There is a list of items with prices, but the items are random—bacon, bacon-lard, pork-fat, iron, sundries—though the prices do provide information on relative values. A similar style of list includes overcoats, pepper, towels, tallow, and thongs; a third, lees of wine, barley, wagon-axles, and wheat. One result of all these lists is that we now know both the price of many items and that the Romans could calculate in fractions down to an eighth of a *denarius* (Figure 2). The details revealed by these documents illustrate the military bureaucracy at work, supported by a receipt from elsewhere which was issued in quadruplicate!

The documents were mostly prepared by the clerks who worked in the rooms at the rear of the headquarters building. To each side of the central room, which contained the statue of the emperor and the standards of the unit, lay two rooms. In some cases, one room could only be entered through that beside it and it may be that the officer in charge of the clerical staff occupied the inner room (Figure 17). The Vindolanda writing tablets were, however, found in and beside the commanding officer's house, many having survived a bonfire. They include far more than lists, including copies of letters sent by the commanding officer, requests for leave, and documents concerning the administration of the units stationed at the fort. It is probable that they were prepared in the commanding officer's own office.

Clerks undertook this form of record-keeping in every fort of the Empire. Other actions such as the requisition and ordering of army supplies were carried out at a higher level. Documents from the eastern provinces of the Empire record that the village of Terton Epa supplied one army unit with 100 *artabas* of barley as part of the order for 20,000 *artabas* from the Prefect of Egypt to the Hermopolite district (the price of one *artaba* of wheat as fixed by the state in 155 was 2 *denarii*; this order was therefore worth 40,000 *denarii*). In 138, advance payments were authorized to weavers of the village of Philadelphia for clothing that the Prefect of Egypt had ordered to be manufactured for the army in Cappadocia—one tunic, four Syrian cloaks, one blanket for the hospital, with detailed specifications given for the clothing. Weavers in Egypt also supplied nineteen tunics and five cloaks to the army of Judaea in 128. Still in the second century, 200 and 775 blankets were the subject of separate purchases by the army of Egypt. Several of these orders crossed a provincial boundary and emphasize the reach of the army and its considerable importance in the local economy.

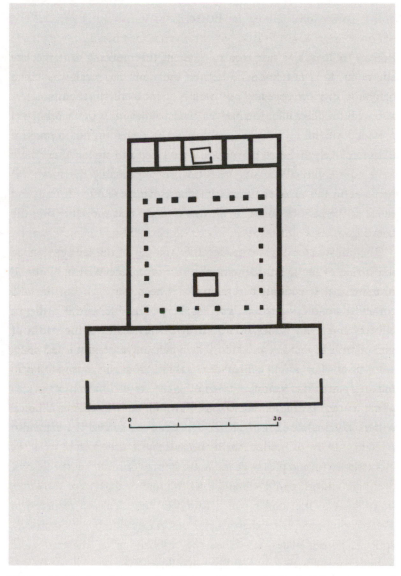

Figure 17 The headquarters building at Newstead. This building consists of four elements. At the back (top on the plan) lie the four rooms of the regimental clerks flanking the central temple where the standards of the units were displayed above a strongroom. In front is a cross-hall probably used for assemblies and beyond that is a courtyard surrounded by a veranda; possibly notices were pinned up here. Across the entrance (bottom on the plan) is a large hall of the type used for training under cover.

Food

Roman soldiers had two meals a day, in the morning and the late afternoon. It is not known whether the morning meal was taken before or after the parade. Food was brought to the fort, but soldiers also went to collect it for themselves. Each soldier, in theory at least, was provided with his own rations and cooked his own food, but in practice it is more likely that each barrack-room cooked and ate together. There were no communal messing facilities, so presumably the food was prepared in the lee of the rampart, where ovens are often found, and eaten in the barrack-room or on the veranda that ran alongside the building.

The range of food was considerable. Analysis of the sewage outside the latrine of the fort at Bearsden on the Antonine Wall in Scotland revealed that it contained remains of wheat, barley, bean, fig, dill, coriander, opium poppy, hazelnut, raspberry, bramble, wild strawberry, bilberry, and celery. Bones did not survive here because of the acidity of the soil. Wheat could be used to make bread, porridge, pasta, and soup; one type of wheat found at Bearsden was macaroni wheat used today in making pasta. The Vindolanda writing tablets include references to wheat, barley, bread, lentils, lovage, radishes, olives, meal, fish-sauce, oysters, gruel, apples, eggs, honey, oil, pepper, and spices. There are also references to the ox herds at the wood and pigs.

Cattle, sheep, and pigs were the main sources of meat, but the flesh of deer, hare, and other wild animals, fowl, fish, and shellfish were also eaten. In addition to the food remains found at Bearsden and recorded at Vindolanda, pears, plums, cherries, peaches, grapes, elderberries, damsons, apricots, pomegranates, lentils, carrots, cabbage, peas, chestnuts, and walnuts have all been found on Roman military sites.

Quern stones and mill stones appear to have been owned communally, as some are marked with the name of the barrack-room or the century. Wheat and barley was prepared in mixing bowls, which are very common in British forts and again are sometimes marked with the name of a barrack-room.

Both wine and beer were drunk; at Vindolanda there is a reference to Celtic beer and to a brewer, wine, sour wine and Massic wine, a better quality wine probably drunk by the officers. Aqueducts are known at some forts; settling tanks might have been used to help purify the water.

Some items of food travelled considerable distances. Olive oil, wine, and fish-based products came to Britain from Spain, wine and certain types of pottery from southern France, while figs, coriander, and opium poppy also came from the Mediterranean littoral.

Health

All forts except the smallest appear to have contained a hospital and each unit a doctor. The medical staff in a legion was naturally larger than in an auxiliary unit and included medical assistants, ointment makers, and bandagers, while an administrative officer was in charge of the hospital and cavalry units had vets. Medical supplies were required. Some plants used for medicinal purposes were grown in the courtyard of the hospital. Remains of celery, which was used for medicinal purposes in antiquity, were found at Bearsden. Ointments are known, in particular for the eyes; as has been mentioned, conjunctivitis was a common problem in the army. A certificate of discharge dating to 52 records that a certain Tryphon, son of Dionysius, weaver, was discharged with weak sight owing to a cataract following an examination in Alexandria in Egypt. Although it is not clear that the man was a soldier, the document suggests that such certificates were used in the army.

Two other important buildings were the bath house and the latrine (Figure 18). The former, usually placed outside the fort, obviously aided cleanliness, but it was also a place where the soldiers could relax. In many bath houses there was a choice of bathing: the steam treatment known today as the Turkish bath (so named because the Turks took over the Roman baths when they conquered the Eastern Roman Empire) and the hot dry treatment or sauna. After each type of bathing, the soldier would then complete the process by stepping into the cold bath.

Figure 18 The bath house and latrine at Bearsden looking south. Along the spine of the building from right to left lie the changing room, cold room, and three warm rooms with the furnace far left. To the near side of the cold room is the hot dry room and beyond it is the cold bath. A hot bath is placed next to the hot steam room and furnace. Top left is the latrine, flushed by water carried from the bath house by drains. Bottom left is part of an early bath house.

Each fort contained at least one communal latrine, usually located at the lower end of the site where it could use the water flowing downhill. The sewage itself passed under the fort wall and debouched into the fort ditch; at Bearsden, the outer ditch was half full of rotting sewage when the fort was abandoned. Analysis of this was a rich source of information about the diet of the soldiers at this fort, and included an indication that the balance of their diet was mainly plant based.

The Romans did not, of course, understand about the causes of diseases in the modern way. Hence, in Roman houses a latrine was often placed next to the kitchen, something that would be frowned upon today. But they did understand the need to provide this basic facility and get rid of the noxious material. Roman latrines are much admired, but excavations in the fort at Carlisle have revealed a different aspect.

Human waste was found within the fort together with moss, which could have been used for cleaning. It would appear that soldiers did not make it to the latrine on time or merely defecated elsewhere, as the graffiti on the walls of Pompeii stating "do not defecate here" imply happened within that city. Other environmental evidence from Carlisle suggests that large numbers of flies and other insects bred in what appear to have been puddles of rotting waste in some parts of the fort, and these could have carried diseases such as salmonella and typhoid and caused diarrhea. This archaeological evidence challenges the normal view of the hygienic Romans with flush-water latrines and hospitals.

Duties

At times when examining Roman military documents one wonders when soldiers found the time to fight. In the fort, as we have seen, soldiers had to undertake guard duty. This was not restricted to the standards in the headquarters building but included the gates of the fort, the main road junctions within the fort, the commander's residence, the granaries, and the artillery depot. The changing of the guards was marked by a blast of the horn.

Other soldiers would be involved in repairing the fort or building other military installations. Soldiers collected supplies and guarded their transport. Some spent time away from their base serving in the governor's bodyguard. There was a steady correspondence between unit commander and provincial governor with soldiers carrying letters to and fro. Prisoners needed guarding. Indeed, as there was no police force in the Roman world, soldiers were often employed to help keep the peace and support the law officers. Mines for precious metals such as silver and gold were owned by the state, and soldiers might be employed guarding the miners who were slaves. In some provinces, soldiers collected taxes, or actually were the taxes themselves, as the Batavians are recorded as having to provide recruits rather than money. As frontiers developed during the later first and second centuries, many men were outposted to man fortlets and towers and to supervise points of entry to the Empire. Here, their duties included preventing raiding and enforcing the regulations that governed entry to the Empire; people could only come in unarmed, at specified points, and proceed under military escort.

There were also special parades, such as the pay parades. These were more than merely the occasion when money was paid and banked, for they served another important purpose. Pliny, when governor of Bithynia and Pontus under the reign of Trajan, wrote to inform the emperor that the annual vows to ensure his safety and therefore that of the Empire had been made; this occurred on the first pay-day of the year 112. On January 28, the anniversary of Trajan's accession, Pliny offered prayers to the gods and administered the oath of allegiance to the troops under his command.

A fragmentary document known as the Feriale Duranum, found at Dura and dating to about 225, covers the period from January 1 to September 23 when it breaks off. It lists no less than forty-one religious festivals for those nine months; if the pattern continued, then the total for the year would be about fifty-four. The form of the festival is similar in each case: the occasion is stated—for example, the anniversary of the emperor's accession or the birthday of a previous emperor—with the appropriate sacrifice (a bull, an ox or a cow), and the name of the god(s) or goddess(es) to whom it is made.

Hadrian was an unusual emperor because he toured the provinces and inspected his armies. Knowledge of some of the events that occurred during his inspections survives, including a remarkable display by a soldier on the Danube (see p. 32) and the record of some of his speeches in North Africa. These may have been special occasions but it is clear that there were other military displays when cavalrymen wore "sports" masks and undertook complicated exercises (Figure 19). Some of these are recorded for us, not least by Arrian, governor of Cappadocia under Hadrian. He stated that the exercises should take place on a level field in which a square was marked out with the turf broken up to provide a soft and springy surface. One exercise involved throwing lances at a target from horseback, including one while turning

Figure 19 The Crosby Garrett helmet was found in 2010 in Cumbria. It is a superb example of the cavalry "sports" helmet made for use in mock combat.

the horse, while others entailed the firing of sling shot and artillery. Mock battles might be fought. The exercises commented upon by Hadrian included the building of practice camps.

While Hadrian might have been unusual, his governors certainly undertook regular inspections and kept a close watch on their provinces. In addition to his other books, Arrian has left an account of his tour of inspection round the eastern shore of the Black Sea. He visited each fort, recorded the strength of the unit based there, and took measures to improve its defense if necessary.

It was important to keep the soldiers busy. According to Tacitus, when Corbulo took up command on the eastern frontier in 58, he found old soldiers who had never served on watch or guard duty, who did not own a helmet of a breastplate, and who lived in town not in the fort. Perhaps there was hyperbole in the anecdote, but when he was governor of Lower Germany under Claudius he had his men dig a canal between the Meuse and the Saône in order to keep them busy.

Decorations

The Roman army had a wide range of decorations to hand out to its officers and soldiers. Rather as in today's British army, the decorations often related to one's rank. Those awarded to the soldiers were necklaces (*torques*), armbands (*armillae*), and discs, rather like large medals, worn on the cuirass (*phalerae*). Officers could be awarded miniature flags. Some decorations, however, were awarded irrespective of rank. These included the siege crown to the soldier responsible for raising a siege, the civic crown for saving the life of a Roman citizen, the mural crown for being the first to scale the walls of an enemy city, and another for being the first over the rampart of an enemy camp, the naval crown, and the gold crown.

Honorific titles like "loyal", "faithful" or "martial" might be granted to units and in special cases a whole auxiliary regiment might be awarded Roman citizenship, which would then be added to their title. Some units acquired very long titles, such as the First Cohort of Breuci, five hundred strong, part mounted, styled Valiant and Victorious for valour, twice awarded necklaces.

Decorations were awarded not just as a result of special service in warfare, but for faithfulness in a rebellion; Domitian gave the title of faithful to all the units of Lower Germany for remaining loyal during the rebellion of Saturninus in 89. As today, some emperors were more generous than others in their awards.

Punishments

As we have seen (p. 21), punishments could be severe under the generals of the Republic. The most severe punishment of decimation died out during the first century AD, the last recorded instance being in 68. Desertion, mutiny, and insubordination could be punished by death, but this was rarely carried out, consideration being given to the particular circumstances of the case. Soldiers might be discharged dishonorably, reduced in rank, fined or flogged. Augustus is recorded as ordering centurions to stand all day outside the commander's tent not wearing armor or a belt—that is, as if they were civilians—and sometimes holding a measuring pole or a turf block.

In extreme circumstances, a unit might be disbanded. The three legions lost in the Varian disaster were not re-formed; the surviving soldiers were deployed elsewhere and the numbers of the legions were not used again. After the Batavian Revolt of 69–70, two legions were reformed into a single legion with a new name, while in the third century two legions were disbanded, not because of a military disgrace but rather for opposing the emperor of the day.

Leave

Leave is an almost unknown element of the soldiers' life. Under Augustus, legionaries had to pay their centurions for the right to have leave, but the emperor Otho later took over this responsibility. Several letters at Vindolanda are requests for leave: "I, Messicus . . . ask, my lord, that you consider me a worthy person to whom to grant leave at *Coria*"—that is, Corbridge, a few miles to the east. It would appear that leave was not a right, but how often it was granted remains unknown.

Slaves

Roman soldiers owned slaves. These might be owned individually, or by a group of soldiers. It is not known what these slaves did or where they lived. Perhaps they cooked for the soldiers and groomed the horses. The tombstones of some cavalrymen show a slave walking behind the soldier carrying his spears.

Family life

Soldiers were not allowed to marry according to Roman law until about 200. That did not prevent them from forming relationships with women and in these circumstances it is clear that many men saw themselves as married. Indeed, such relationships were acknowledged on retirement in so far as auxiliary soldiers were awarded "the right of marriage with the wife they had when citizenship was given to them". One result of the law was that the state did not have to pay for the transport of the soldiers' families when they moved.

Because such relationships produced children, a problem arose. Documents in Egypt show that soldiers who had children when still in the army could make a declaration of paternity to ensure that the child could inherit his or her father's property. In 119, Hadrian affirmed that while children who were born and acknowledged during military service were not the legitimate heirs of the fathers, they should be allowed to claim possession of his property. The crucial point is that while soldiers before the time of Severus could not marry according to

Roman law, they still had relationships that were acknowledged by the state when necessary. It has been suggested that steady unions tended not to occur until some time after the soldier had enlisted, perhaps not until he had been promoted and therefore had more pay.

We have already seen (p. 47) that Scipio Aemilianus is reputed to have thrown 2,000 prostitutes out of the camp at Numantia when he took over the command of the army in the second century BC. From the time of Caligula (37–41), prostitutes had to be registered and were taxed on their earnings, the tax being collected by soldiers. Again, Egypt provides examples of the presence and activities of prostitutes. One letter, written by a prostitute, stated that she had refused to go with a prospective client "for love of a Dacian", while another letter recorded that a soldier sent his wife to the fortlet at *Didymoi* (Khasm-el-Menih) "so that her charms may pay off a debt".

There were, of course, other, hopefully more stable, relationships. Soldiers might have other family members than wives: mothers, mothers-in-law, and sisters are recorded on tombstones along the frontiers of the Empire. Inscriptions suggest that many sons of soldiers joined their fathers' regiment in due course.

All such people—and more—lived in the settlement outside the fort, where in addition to dwellings, there were shops, temples, and baths. But the folk of the settlement were not necessarily excluded from the fort. A lady called Belica appears to have kept a tavern within the legionary base at Vindonissa in Switzerland, and her clientele might have embraced other activities too. It may be that civilians could have gone into the fort during the day though were excluded, at least in theory, at night.

Corruption

A soldier was a powerful figure in society, able to apply pressure on his fellow citizens. In 238, the villagers of Skaptopara in Thrace (modern Bulgaria) complained that soldiers forced them to provide hospitality and supplies free of charge, while the complaints of Arague in Asia (modern Turkey) in 244–247 included extortion, pillage, attacks and beatings, and the theft of plough animals. A list of expenses drawn up by an agent for his master in the third or fourth century included the cost of wine for bribes to soldiers on several occasions. When soldiers, perhaps those of King Herod rather than the Roman army, asked John the Baptist what they should do, he replied, "do not extort money from anyone, do not act as an informer, and be satisfied with your pay", thereby listing precisely how the soldiers did act!

This somewhat bleak picture of corruption caught the attention of the literary world of Rome. In a scene in Petronius' *Satyricon*, written in the first century, the hero was robbed by a soldier. Juvenal wrote his satire on *The Advantages of Army Life* during the reign of Hadrian, that great friend of the Roman army. He said,

> … consider the advantages shared by all soldiers, not least being the fact that no civilian would dare to beat you up, and if he himself is beaten he will try to keep it quiet. He will not dare to show the judge the gaps in his teeth, the black lumps and the swollen bruises on his face, the one eye left, about which the doctor offers little hope. If he seeks redress, a hob-nailed judge is assigned to the case.

Finally, later in the second century in his fantastical novel, *The Golden Ass*, Apuleius described a scene in which a market gardener riding an ass met a centurion who demanded the animal. As he spoke in Latin, the market gardener did not understand, so the centurion hit him with his vine-stick and repeated the demand in Greek; the market gardener fought back, but after further adventures the centurion managed to obtain the ass. In short, the lesson was that if you saw a Roman soldier coming towards you, it was wise to cross the street.

Corruption occurred throughout the hierarchy. The taxation of the Frisii across the North Sea is a case in point. In the middle of the first century, one Roman officer, Olennius by name, was imaginative in his interpretation of the payment of taxes in the form of hides, producing the hide of a wild ox and using this as the standard. The Frisii sought to meet the demand, selling their cattle, then their lands, and finally their wives and children, before rising in rebellion; the Romans lost over a thousand soldiers before the revolt was quashed.

Roman authorities sought to deal with corruption. Throughout the first century, prefects of Egypt issued edicts forbidding illegal actions by soldiers. In the reign of Hadrian, the prefect stated in a decree,

> I have learned that many soldiers travel about the country without written requisition, demanding ships, beasts of burden and persons beyond anything authorized, sometimes seizing them by force, sometimes receiving items by favor … abusing and threatening private citizens with the result that the military is associated with arrogance and injustice. I therefore order my officers not to provide travelling facilities to anyone without a certificate, whether moving by river or by land, and will punish severely anyone acting otherwise.

In the next century, Ulpian recorded a law which stated that provincial governors should prevent soldiers unjustly claiming personal advantages for themselves as opposed to taking actions for the benefit of the army as a whole.

Emperors took other steps to seek to prevent abuse and stop corruption. The former included sexual abuse. The somewhat suspect source, the *Augustan History*, records two such episodes both dating to the third century in which emperors took action. Macrinus punished soldiers who had sex with a slave and Aurelian a soldier who committed adultery; in both cases, the soldiers were billeted in the houses where the offences occurred. Yet the mere fact that decrees against abuse continued to be issued demonstrates how difficult it was to stamp it out. This was no doubt partly because it could extend to the highest levels. Governors and procurators could themselves be corrupt, as demonstrated by a document from Africa, which reveals that the procurator of the imperial estates used soldiers to arrest and torture tenants and beat Roman citizens.

The Vindolanda writing tablets provide an example from closer to home. One document is a letter of complaint by a man from overseas at his treatment by soldiers when he was beaten; unfortunately, we do not know the nature of the official to whom he complained. The action is strikingly similar to St. Paul's complaint as recorded in *The Acts of the Apostles*. Paul was beaten and then pointed out that the action was illegal because he was a Roman citizen and thereafter applied for redress to the emperor. The *New Testament* is a useful source of information about the actions of Roman soldiers in relation to their fellow citizens.

Promotion

For several years, most soldiers would undertake general fatigues in addition to their regular training. But they could also specialize and/or seek promotion (Table 2). Each unit contained men who were termed *immunes*—that is, men immune from general fatigues; soldiers normally had to serve for three to four years before obtaining such a post. A list of *immunes* included surveyors, medical orderlies, craftsmen, ditchers, farriers, architects, pilots, shipwrights, artillery-makers, glaziers, smiths, arrow-makers, copper-smiths, wagon-makers, sword-cutlers, water-engineers, trumpet-makers, horn-makers, bow-makers, butchers, hunters, priests, clerks, grooms, tanners, weapon-keepers, heralds, and trumpeters.

Two letters of Julius Apollinarius illustrate the way such a post might be obtained. In one letter to his father written on March 26, 107, he

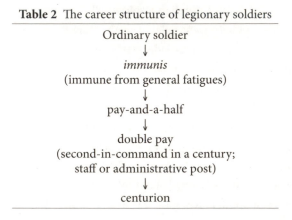

Table 2 The career structure of legionary soldiers

Ordinary soldier
↓
immunis
(immune from general fatigues)
↓
pay-and-a-half
↓
double pay
(second-in-command in a century;
staff or administrative post)
↓
centurion

stated that he had asked the governor of the province to appoint him a clerk on his staff. The governor replied that there was no vacancy but he offered Apollinarius a post in the legion of which he was also commander. In the second letter, to his mother probably written in the following year, he tells her that while everyone is toiling cutting stones, he walks around doing nothing.

There was obviously an advantage to such a post, but it brought no extra pay. For this, a soldier had to become a *principalis*, a junior officer, which usually didn't occur until after at least six years' service. There were two grades of *principales* below the rank of centurion and decurion: one received pay-and-a-half and the other double pay. The more senior grade included the standard bearer and the second-in-command of the century as well as the senior staff of the commander's office.

By the end of the first century (if not before), a career structure had developed for junior officers. If they sought promotion to centurion or decurion, they normally had to hold three or four posts embracing both administrative and tactical positions so that they gained experience of all aspects of army life—and bureaucracy. Each would be held for about three years and the culmination was the post of *optio ad spem ordinis*, the second-in-command of the century or troop who had been marked out for promotion to centurion or decurion (literally, second-in-command with hope of promotion to centurion). The advancement to centurion or decurion usually happened between the thirteenth and twentieth year, though exceptional soldiers could pass quickly through the ranks. Of course, not all soldiers were promoted to be a centurion or decurion; those that did not remained in the ranks, experienced in all the army's multifarious activities.

Officers

Today, we are used to referring to the officers and the men. In the Roman army, there were three main groups, the senior officers, the centurionate, and the men. The senior officers were aristocrats, at first from Rome, but increasingly from the provinces. Most centurions had risen through the ranks (Figure 9); some achieved the distinction of obtaining higher posts. The men were volunteers, but had the opportunity for advancement through service in the army.

The commanders of the legions and their seconds-in-command were members of the senatorial class, the upper aristocracy, while the junior tribunes in the legions and the commanders of the auxiliary units were drawn from the equestrian order or knights, the lower aristocracy (Table 3). The commander of the legion was a senator, in his thirties, en route to a consulship and provincial governorship(s). His second-in-command was a tribune, a young man from the same social class in his first military post. It is probable that both served for a period of three years. Immediately below them was the prefect of the camp. He was a professional soldier, a former centurion with many years of experience. He was the man who really ran the legion. There were also five junior tribunes, men from the lower aristocratic class, the equestrians or knights, in their second post in a military career that might take them on to the command of a fleet or even of the Praetorian Guard in Rome. The centurions were the backbone of the legion, most with at least thirteen years in the ranks and who could continue in service for decades. They were supported by junior officers and soldiers with special responsibilities, as we have seen.

Table 3 The career structure of senators

Magistrate in Rome, aged 18/19
↓
Senior tribune in a legion, aged 20
↓
Magistrate in Rome, aged 25+, and a senator
↓
Legionary legate/governor of a small province, aged 30+
↓
Consul, aged 33+
↓
Governor of a senior province

Table 4 The career structure of commanders of auxiliary units

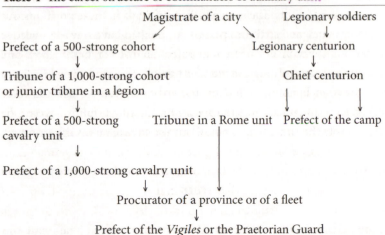

The commander of an auxiliary unit was a knight who entered the army in his thirties after playing a role in governing his own city, and he began by commanding the smallest auxiliary unit before moving up the grades until, if successful, he commanded one of the thousand-strong cavalry units, of which there were only ten in the Empire (Table 4). There were fewer posts at each successive level, so the unsatisfactory officers could be weeded out. Those who reached the top level might eventually command one of the provincial fleets or govern a small province.

There were two entry points to the centurionate. As we have seen, most were promoted from the ranks, but a direct commission was also possible. A provincial magistrate seeking a military career had to consider carefully the pros and cons of each type of appointment. If he sought a post as the commander of an auxiliary unit, he would have greater prestige, but more uncertainty of promotion. On the other hand, the less important post of centurion might give him a career for life, as there was no retirement age and it is known that some centurions served for over fifty years.

A provincial governor had the authority to appoint centurions and the lowest grade of auxiliary commanders, though imperial approval had then to be sought; the emperor himself was responsible for all senior appointments. The number of individuals in these positions was relatively small and so the emperor was likely to have some knowledge of many of them. In an emergency, such as an invasion or rebellion, care was taken to choose the right man for the job. Thus, in 132 or 133, when there was an uprising in Judaea, the man selected to lead the force tasked to restore order was the governor of Britain, Julius Severus; he had to cross the entire length of the Empire to take up his appointment.

Retirement

Under the Republic, soldiers might serve for sixteen years and this continued to be the term of service of the Praetorian Guard in Rome. By the time of Augustus, the length of service of legionaries was twenty years. It was later increased to twenty-five—actually, twenty-five or twenty-six, because the discharge process appears to have operated every other year. Legionaries had earlier received land on retirement but this was commuted, at least by the early second century, into a sum of money. Auxiliary soldiers were granted Roman citizenship.

Many soldiers did not return to the home that they had left twenty-five years earlier, instead settling locally, perhaps having found a local wife. Some may simply have moved out of the fort into the adjacent civil settlement. A comparison of the life expectancy of soldiers and civilians suggested that the former had better prospects until retirement when, perhaps after the regular pay and food of the army had ceased, their life expectancy dropped below that of civilians of comparable age.

6

Arms and Armor

They were all heavy armed troops and had helmets, cuirasses, greaves and shields.

Vegetius, *Epitome of Military Science*, 2, 15

Every soldier would have had the following arms and armor: helmet, body armor, skirt, tunic, knee breeches, underclothes, belt, sword, dagger, shield and shield cover, spears, shoes and probably socks, and cloak. Musicians and standard bearers had special requirements, animal skins of bear, lion, and wolf. Centurions wore greaves. Some units used bows and arrows. Horses required saddles, bridles and bits, straps, and so on. In addition, the troops need practice weapons, spears and darts, wooden swords, and to these we can add for parades and exercises, helmet crests, shields and, for some, face masks (Figure 19). These total an incredibly large number of items and the fact that all soldiers were suitably equipped demonstrates the efficiency of the Roman supply system.

Legionaries

In the time of Augustus, both legionaries and auxiliaries wore mail shirts, though scale armor is known to be have been worn also. A new form of cuirass was, however, introduced at this time, dated by the discovery of part of one at the site of the Battle of the Teutoberg Forest in AD 9. The cuirass was formed of horizontal iron plates fixed to leather straps and was similar to a jacket in that it was put on the body and then fastened at the front. Vertical strips protected the shoulders, which were especially vulnerable in battle. This armor is known as the *lorica segmentata*, though the term is modern.

The cuirass was worn over a simple tunic usually of wool or linen, likely usually white in color, sometimes with sleeves, and held tight by a belt. Some form of padding lay between the tunic and the armor to prevent chafing. Sometimes two or more belts were worn, the sword attached to one and a dagger to the other. An apron was usually attached to a belt at the front to protect the genitals, at least during the first and second centuries. The belts were often highly ornamented. They were also important because the military belt marked out a soldier who was not wearing his armor. A cloak, held by a brooch on the left side, fell over the soldier's shoulders.

The helmet was ingeniously created to protect the head (Figure 20). It was in the form of a hemisphere, with cheek pieces to each side tied at the front, a strip of metal sticking out on each side to protect the ears,

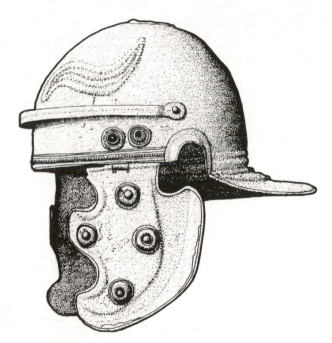

Figure 20 A legionary helmet demonstrating the protection provided to the cheeks, the ears, and the nose.

a neck guard at the back, and a projecting flange at the front to stop a downward blow cutting off the nose. The helmet was surmounted by a crest. One purpose of the crest was to suggest that the soldier was taller than he actually was and thereby intimidate the enemy.

The military boot was well designed to grip, its sole being heavily studded. This provided for excellent grip on grass, but could cause problems on hard surfaces, as a soldier in Jerusalem found in 70 when he slipped and fell on paving stones and was killed.

The legionary shield was rectangular and semi-circular in shape. It was formed of three layers of thin wood glued together at right angles to each other, with the edges of the shield protected by metal binding. In the center was a metal boss, which protected the hand grip. Some bosses were highly decorated, while the shield itself was painted with various designs. When not in use, it was protected by a leather cover.

Legionaries were equipped with a throwing-spear with a soft shank that would bend on impact and therefore be useless to the enemy (*pilum*), and a short-stabbing sword known as the *gladius* (Figure 21).

©aga

Figure 21 A relief of legionaries from Croy on the Antonine Wall. This would appear to be a father and his two sons; note the *pilum* (spear).

This sword, being short, was worn on the right side and could be easily extracted from its sheath.

Auxiliary soldiers

The auxiliary infantryman wore a mail shirt of iron rings and a helmet of iron or bronze. His shield was oval and flat, made of plywood covered with leather with a circular metal boss and metal rim. He was equipped with a spear for throwing or thrusting and a sword, a version of the short stabbing sword of the legionary. It was 600 mm long and 50 mm wide, designed for thrusting with its long point, but it also had cutting edges. A dagger was also carried.

The cavalrymen wore mail shirts that were adapted for their use by the insertion of a slit on each side to make it easier to sit on a horse. Their swords were longer because, sitting on a horse, a cavalryman was further from the enemy. Their helmets were usually more ornate than those of the infantry.

Other soldiers in the army appear to have worn little protective armor. On Trajan's Column appear slingers holding their stones in the fold of their tunic, clubmen wearing trousers but fighting bare to the waist, and Moorish light cavalry wearing tunics (Figures 22 and 23).

Adaptation to local conditions

The Roman army started its life in the Mediterranean but as it met new enemies and made new conquests, it both adopted items of arms and armor from its enemies, such as the helmet, and adapted its own armor to the different climatic conditions. The Vindolanda writing tablets offer an excellent example of the latter, for one letter home records a soldier being sent pairs of socks, two pairs of sandals, and two pairs of underpants. Breeches were worn on the cold northern frontier, and a long cloak with a hood might be worn, rather like a duffle cloak but without sleeves.

Figure 22 Legionaries march toward the battle, while ahead is a slinger and a clubman, though unfortunately his club has been removed from his hand. To the far left is an auxiliary soldier in a mail shirt.

Standard bearers

We have already observed the important role of the standard bearers (pp. 55–6). Their armor reflected this; some wore scale armor rather than mail or the legionary cuirass. The standard bearers also wore animal skins. The legionary standard bearers had bear skins while the praetorian standard bearers had lion skins. The heads of these animals covered the soldiers' helmets to give them a more terrifying appearance.

Officers

Distinguishing officers from ordinary soldiers was achieved in different ways. Caesar was identified by the color of his cloak. According to the Elder Pliny, generals had scarlet cloaks. Other officers may have worn blue cloaks, while those of the soldiers were red or brown. Red is a fairly

Figure 23 Moorish cavalry riding bareback depicted on Trajan's Column. None wears armor, but each carries an oval shield. These soldiers were recruited from the frontier tribes of North Africa.

common color at Vindolanda, while dyeing wool blue is more difficult. The crest might be used to mark officers; centurions, for example, wore theirs at right angles to those of ordinary soldiers.

The provision of arms and armor

The *Notitia Dignitatum* records arms factories under the command of a senior officer. Factories specialized in the production of shields, weapons, arrows, bows, body armor, artillery, spears or a combination of up to three of these. A law of 344 refers to state boot factories that may have supplied the army. These records, however, refer to the fourth century. Earlier documents appear to suggest that the army ordered clothing, if not armor, from civilians. In the first decade of the second century, soldiers from the First Cohort of Spaniards based in a fort on the Lower Danube were in Gaul collecting clothing, while the armies of Cappadocia and Judaea ordered clothing from Egypt. The purchase of such supplies from civilians continued into the fourth century when a document records payments by soldiers to the tailor, the fuller, the smith, for tunics, and for a shield cover.

We can see that merchants made substantial profits out of supplying the army. In 301, Diocletian published a price edict stipulating the maximum prices to be paid for goods. He drew attention to the exaggerated prices charged, noting that:

> ...sometimes in a single retail sale a soldier is stripped of his donative and pay. Moreover, the contributions of the whole world for the support of the armies fall as profits into the hands of these plunderers, and our soldiers appear to bestow with their own hands the rewards of their military service and their veterans' bonuses upon the profiteers.

Many forts contained a workshop, perhaps more for the repair than the manufacture of arms and armor. The legionary fortress, however, usually contained a large workshop. Excavation of the workshop at

Exeter recovered defective castings from the production of metal objects as well as evidence for a lathe. The army contained in its own ranks artillery-makers, smiths, arrow-makers, sword-cutlers, trumpet-makers, horn-makers, bow-makers, as well as weapon-keepers.

It seems that the soldiers could also obtain their own arms, armor, and clothing. A recruit to the fleet, writing to his father in the early second century, asked him to send him clothes and equipment to avoid having to pay for new ones. A few years later, a cavalryman borrowed 50 *denarii* from a private individual to help pay for arms, the money to be repaid from his salary. Another soldier's letter to his family included a request for a tunic, trousers, and a cloak. By the fourth century, recruits were given 6 *solidi* to cover the cost of their uniforms and other items provided by the state. Receipts dated to the fourth century record payments by soldiers for tunics and a shield cover. Perhaps the soldiers did not have to travel far for their purchases, since in a letter to his father sent in 107, Iulius Apollinaris stated that the merchants came to his fort at Bostra every day.

Several documents indicate that on death or retirement, arms and armor (and the soldier's share of the tent) would be sold or passed on. Sometime in the reign of Hadrian, Dionysius, a cavalryman in an unknown Egyptian unit, withdrew 1458 *denarii* from his military account and received an additional 103 *denarii* for his arms, presumably on his retirement. In another example, in 143 a mother received the money left by her deceased son, Ammonius, formerly a soldier in the Second Cohort of Thracians in Egypt, which included one sum for weapons and another for a tent; she collected the money from the unit's headquarters building. The tent would obviously have to be surrendered, for this was shared with his comrades in the barrack-room, but the document suggests that it was owned communally. The weapons were presumably sold. There are relatively few burials containing military equipment uncovered in the Roman Empire but this is not surprising if the arms and armor were sold on. Items of military equipment are known bearing several names; these include helmets, swords, a shield boss and a greave, one marked with as many as five names. As in so much, the Romans were a pragmatic people.

Cavalrymen obviously required a horse. Documents from Syria demonstrate the procedure of acquiring one. The prefect of the Twentieth Cohort of Palmyrenes applied to the governor of his province for horses for individual soldiers and the governor duly authorized the issue of identified horses to named soldiers. The price of each horse was 125 *denarii*. In the fourth century, the charge to the soldier for his horse was 7 *solidi*, even though the price paid by the state might be as high as 23 *solidi*.

7

The Army as Builders

*Count Equitius ordered the construction of a tower which was
carried out by the Lauriacensian auxiliaries.*

ILS 774

Camps

Accounts of campaigning during the Republic make reference to camps
constructed to protect the Roman army overnight. Those still visible at
Renieblas and Numantia, erected in the middle years of the second
century BC, are a good example (Figure 5).

Vegetius, writing in the late fourth century, offered rules for
encampment. The most advantageous place should be found, to stop
the enemy from occupying it; and it should not be overlooked by higher
ground nearby. It should not be on low ground where it could be
flooded. In the summer it should not be near bad water or far from
good, and should be close to forage and to wood. The best dimensions
for a camp were that its length be one-third greater than its width, and
the size of the camp should be carefully calculated by the surveyors so
that it was appropriate for the force to occupy it. The camp should be
defended by a slight rampart of turf planted with stakes and fronted
by a ditch, at least five Roman feet broad and three deep (1.5 meters ×
1 meter); the same measurements were specified by pseudo-Hyginus.
Caltrops or tree trunks with sharpened branches might be used for
further defense beyond the ditch.

Soldiers in peacetime practised building such temporary camps.
Groups of these are known in Wales and some also along Hadrian's

Wall. They are all small and with an entrance on each side, indicating that the soldiers concentrated on the difficult elements, the rounded corners, the defensive function of which is mentioned by pseudo-Hyginus, and protection of the gate.

Caesar's *Gallic War* includes brief mention of winter quarters. The army was split up and quartered in friendly territory, presumably partly to ease supply. Within the camps, the soldiers erected timber huts with thatched roofs, which Caesar stated was normal in Gaul.

Forts

At the time of Caesar—that is, the late Republic—references to forts appear to indicate military installations built to control passes or the movement of enemy forces, and which were only occupied during the fighting months and then abandoned. We know nothing of the size or any other details of these structures. Under Augustus, as the army settled down into bases that they began to occupy for some years, they erected forts using turves for the ramparts and timber for the buildings. We should not see these as inferior to stone structures; the Roman soldiers were experienced builders and created sophisticated timber buildings.

Vegetius specified the size of the turf blocks to be used in building a rampart, 450 × 300 × 150 millimeters thick (Figure 24). On excavations today, the black lines of the decayed grass are often still visible. On top of the rampart there was a timber breastwork. A burnt layer, 1.5 meters wide, in front of the rampart of the fort at Bearsden on the Antonine Wall contained thin branches of willow, hazel, and alder, each about 10–15 millimeters in diameter; these presumably had formed part of the timber breastwork.

These particular timbers are relatively soft and therefore the army sought to use a harder wood such as oak for its buildings. Sometimes burning was used to harden the end of timbers inserted into the ground, but mostly the timbers were simply dropped into post-holes. Their life

Figure 24 Legionaries building a fort. The soldiers remove the earth from the ditch in baskets. They carry turves on their shoulders, held in place by a strap or rope. One soldier is having his turf removed, placed on the rampart by a comrade chatting to another soldier. Though their helmets and shields have been placed to one side, the soldiers wear full armor.

span was therefore about twenty to twenty-five years before they needed replacing. A timber fort might be rebuilt whole or in part on a regular basis, though the military practice of demolishing a fort when moving out, even if a new unit was about to arrive, makes it difficult to know whether the replacements were due to rotting or to military redeployment.

Large numbers of trees needed to be felled to create a fort. Substantial timbers about 300 millimeters across would be required for gates (Figure 25), while posts about 100 millimeters square were used in the buildings. Smaller branches were gathered for use as wattle panels between the main uprights to which clay daub was applied.

Eventually, and if the regiment stayed long enough in the fort, the timber buildings were replaced by stone ones (Figure 26). In Britain, this started to happen during the reign of Trajan, fifty to sixty years after the invasion of Britain. We are fortunate that inscriptions record this

Figure 25 The reconstructed timber gate at Baginton of the style built in the first century and early second century.

Figure 26 The reconstructed stone gate at South Shields of the style built in the second half of the second century.

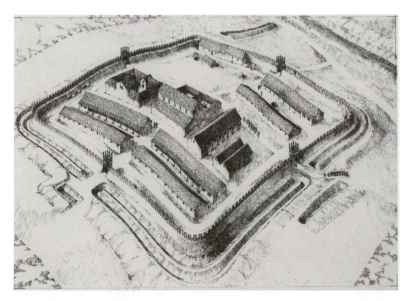

Figure 27 Artist's impression of a fort. This shows the headquarters building in the center of the fort with the commanding officer's house to its left, a granary to the right, and barrack-blocks occupying most of the fort, though with the bath house tucked in behind the rampart top left. Drawn by Michael J. Moore.

work at the legionary bases at Caerleon and York in the first half of Trajan's reign. Although the move to stone continued throughout the province, new forts still tended to be constructed of timber. These included the new legionary base at Carpow on the Tay probably built as late as the reign of Septimius Severus. Here the main buildings were of stone but the barrack-blocks were of timber.

A Roman fort was rather like a small town (Figure 27). The legionary bases were enormous—24 hectares were provided for a single legion—although sometimes two legions were brigaded together. Within the defenses, the buildings were closely packed. The headquarters building was placed in the center, beside the road running across the fort and facing down the main street to the main gate. To each side, and immediately behind, lay the principal and general buildings of the base, the commanding officer's house, houses for the tribunes and other senior officers, hospital, workshop, and sometimes the barrack-blocks of the first cohort. The area in front of the main road across the base and the space behind the central range was normally full of barrack-blocks arranged by cohort and each with its own granary. This general pattern was common to almost every fort, no matter how large or small.

Roman military remains that are visible today show bare walls, but they were not originally like that. The walls, which would have been plastered, sometimes had red lines painted on them to simulate stonework. Painted wall plaster has been discovered inside some buildings, and one barrack-room excavated in Germany had scenes from mythology painted on the interior.

Frontiers

Most of the forts lay on the frontiers of the Empire. Where possible, natural features were used to define the boundaries of the Empire. For most of the southern half of the Empire, the desert offered a convenient boundary, and across the northern frontier the rivers Rhine, Danube, and Euphrates defined the limits of Rome. Mountains in parts of North Africa and in Dacia (modern Romania) formed natural boundaries. In those sectors where no such natural features existed, they were replaced, or supplemented, by linear barriers. These might be of timber, turf, stone or mud-brick, sometimes fronted by a ditch, and normally supplemented by a road linking the forts, fortlets, and towers along their length.

Such barriers had a long history. They were used to try to hem in Spartacus during his rebellion in Italy in the first century BC, and Caesar constructed an earthwork in order to prevent the movement of the Helvetii into Gaul. Some of the later earthworks were similar in principle. In Dacia, valleys that provided access to the province might be blocked by short lengths of rampart and ditch. Under Trajan, an earthwork was constructed across the headwaters of the Rhine and Danube. The most significant campaign, however, was that of Hadrian in the 120s.

In 121, the emperor Hadrian visited Germany and, it would appear, ordered the construction of a palisade along the land frontier of the province. This was formed of substantial timbers, 300 millimeters across, but there was no ditch. He moved on to Britain where a wall of stone (running nearly 80 kilometers) and turf (48 kilometers) was constructed from sea to sea. This was far more substantial than the German palisade. Archaeologists still argue about whether this was required to keep out a fierce enemy, was specially designed by Hadrian himself, perhaps on the basis of the Greek city walls he knew, or was a great symbolic statement of Roman might.

Hadrian's Wall was superseded soon after his death by a new linear barrier in Scotland, the Antonine Wall, this time wholly of turf (apart from the stone buildings in forts). Similarly in Germany, the palisade was replaced. As the timbers decayed, they were replaced by an earthen bank fronted by a ditch. This frontier line was moved forward about 30 kilometers some forty years after it had been built.

In Romania, two barriers crossed the Dobrugea at its narrowest point. The date of these is not known, but one at least is like the Antonine Wall and may be of similar date. Some stretches of this barrier survive; they are a part of what was clearly a substantial bank of earth. The density of forts on this barrier matched that of those on the Antonine Wall, being about 3 kilometers apart.

Finally, in North Africa, relatively short lengths of barriers were identified in the 1940s by French aerial archaeologists and mapped. Some were investigated by excavation and the results published, but they have been little studied since. The barriers certainly exist and gates through them and towers along them have been identified. Pottery from some sites suggests a date in Hadrian's reign, but the military complex has not been studied as an integrated defense system.

The soldiers as builders

The soldiers themselves erected all the buildings. This is illustrated on Trajan's Column where not a single civilian is shown undertaking building work. The soldiers put aside their spears, shields, and helmets, but otherwise labored in full armor because they were in enemy territory (Figure 24). They are shown chopping down trees, erecting buildings, digging ditches, and constructing ramparts. Roman documents and inscriptions inform us that the army contained architects, surveyors, masons, lime-burners, smiths, carpenters, painters, plumbers, and glaziers. In the middle of the second century, Nonius Datus, a surveyor in the Third Augustan Legion in Africa, surveyed a civilian aqueduct at the city of Saldae. The German frontier, erected about 160, runs straight for 81 kilometers without any consideration given to the terrain and with a deviation of just 1 meter; there is no reason to doubt that this was the work of military surveyors. On the Antonine Wall in Scotland, some of the lengths assigned to individual legions were measured to the nearest half pace—another example of precision surveying.

Inscriptions record the construction of Roman military buildings and frontiers by soldiers (Figure 4). Great stone slabs attest to the building of the Antonine Wall in Scotland by soldiers of the three legions of Britain, who also decorated the stones with scenes associated with the prior conquest of Scotland, including the religious ceremony at the start of the campaign, the fighting and the (inevitable) Roman victory. All along Hadrian's Wall simple inscriptions recorded the work of soldiers by century, cohort, and legion, perhaps to facilitate the inspection of the work by senior officers. Individual buildings were decorated by inscriptions recording the emperor and the builder and sometimes the name of the building, such as the headquarters building (*principia*) and its temple (*aedes* or *capitolium*), commanding officer's house (*praetorium*), granary (*horreum*), and bath house (*balneum*).

The Vindolanda writing tablets include several references to soldiers building. On April 25 sometime around the year 100, a total of 343 soldiers were marked as being in the workshops and eighteen building the bath house, with the list also including references to kilns, clay, and plaster. On March 7 one year, thirty soldiers were sent to build 'the residence', nineteen or so to burn stone, and others to produce clay for the wattle fences of the fort.

Ammianus Marcellinus described the army at work in the late fourth century. The emperor of the day, Valentinian, was a great repairer and builder of frontiers. He erected towers, for example, on frontiers from Britain, through Europe to the Near East. He was particularly concerned to protect the Rhine frontier. In order to prevent one of his fortifications being undermined by the River Neckar, he collected men skilled in hydraulic work and began the difficult task with a great number of soldiers. Over many days, beams of oak were bound together and placed in the bed of the river, held together by piles. Although again and again they were swept away by the force of the river, the soldiers finally triumphed over the forces of nature.

This account mentions two important aspects of Roman military constructions: the direction of operations by skilled men and the use of a considerable number of soldiers in the task. Hadrian's Wall is another example of the same practice. Instructions for the Wall itself and the structures along its course were prepared and passed down to each legion, presumably to the office of the prefect of the camp. Here, detailed plans were prepared. Although there was an overall scheme, the structures erected by each of the three legions were distinct. When it came to the construction work, the Wall was simply built. The roughly dressed stones were laid in courses within the minimum of mortar bonding and the interior of the Wall formed of stones and earth. The milecastles were provided with rounded corners, as these were relatively easy to construct for unskilled soldiers. Hadrian's Wall is an excellent example of Roman pragmatism.

The army as manufacturer

Materials of all kinds were required to build a Roman fort, including timber, stone, mortar, clay, thatch, slates, tiles, glass, nails, hinges, locks, and lead pipes. And, of course, tools were required to dig ditches, quarry, break and dress stones, fell and dress timber, and construct buildings. Many of the building materials could be obtained locally—timber, stone, mortar, clay, and thatch. It is unclear whether the owners of these resources were compensated, though it is recorded that Domitian ordered the payment of compensation to farmers who had forts built on their land.

Inscriptions and doodles by Roman soldiers still survive in some of their quarries (Figure 28), and we have already seen Iulius Apollinaris (p. 97) boasting that he was not suffering the fate of his legionary colleagues who spent their days cutting stone in the quarries. The Romans naturally sought building stone appropriate for the task. Quarries flank Hadrian's Wall from which sandstone was extracted; the local hard volcanic rock was much tougher to dress and so was only used in the foundations.

Legions also had kilns for the production of lime operating on a near industrial scale. Soldiers made tiles for their own buildings, on the continent stamping them with the name of the unit, a practice that unfortunately did not take off in Britain. In the first century, the army also made its own pottery, though from the time of Hadrian this was abandoned and replaced by items supplied by civilian manufacturers.

The artifacts found on excavations amplify the picture. The tools of carpenters, masons, and smiths have been found in forts (Figure 29). Many are very similar to the tools used today, as the tasks for which they were employed are the same. As we have seen, the ranks of the army contained many specialists skilled in constructing and maintaining buildings, including surveyors, architects, glaziers, and smiths. Each regiment was, in many ways, a self-contained unit capable of undertaking most of the tasks needed to keep it working effectively.

Figure 28 A soldier's doodle in a quarry near Hadrian's Wall. The inscription records work by a detachment of the Second Legion under the supervision of the *optio* Agricola.

Figure 29 Carpenters' tools. From top left to bottom right: axe, auger, chisel, compasses, file, saw, and two plane blades.

Roads

The army also built the roads that linked all the forts. These were carefully surveyed and often laid out in long straight stretches. The roads themselves were well engineered. A strip of ground was cleared and sometimes a bed of turf was first laid. Over this was a layer of large stones, gradually thinning to a skim of gravel on the surface. Wheel-ruts recorded during excavations indicate that the axle width was about 1.4 meters (the same as the British railway gauge). The roads were flanked by ditches to allow water to disperse. Even today in Scotland some small quarries from which the gravel was extracted to make or re-surface the roads are still visible beside them.

8

The Late Roman Army

Our soldiers during their military service are to be exempt . . . from the normal charges of taxes in kind.

Letter of Constantine to the governor of

Upper Pannonia, 311

On March 21, 235 the emperor Severus Alexander, last of the Severan dynasty, was murdered by his own men. This was followed by fifty years of civil wars and enemy invasions. Nearly forty emperors reigned, some only for months, before Diocletian assumed power in September 284. He reigned for just over twenty years and in that time changed the system of succession, reorganized the administrative structure of the Empire, and reformed the army. After another interlude of turmoil, Constantine became joint emperor in 312 and then sole emperor from 324 to 337. He was another reformer; unfortunately, the inadequacy of our sources does not always allow us correctly to attribute changes to Diocletian or to Constantine. But at the end of this period, a new army had been created.

Warfare occurred on the frontier during every reign from Augustus onwards. For the first 250 years of the Empire, the Romans generally had the upper hand. They even expanded their empire, notably under Claudius, Trajan, and Septimius Severus. But the reign of Marcus Aurelius can be seen as a tipping point. For the first time, there were major invasions of the Empire on two fronts. At the start of the new reign in 161, the Parthians invaded the Roman protectorate of Armenia and annihilated a Roman legion. The co-emperor Lucius Verus went to deal with the crisis and victory was achieved by 166, but the returning soldiers brought back plague. Furthermore, as the emperors were celebrating their triumph in Rome, the first of a series of invasions swept into Pannonia (modern Austria and Hungary) on the northern frontier; warfare was to continue there for fourteen years. Unfortunately for Rome, a new restlessness around its borders resulted in other occasions when warfare raged on two fronts. In 231, for example, Severus Alexander defeated the Sassanians, the new rulers of Parthia, but an invasion of the Alamanni in Germany caused him to break off fighting as success lay within his grasp and rush to Europe to retrieve the situation there. Emperors increasingly shuffled between the eastern and northern frontiers attempting to repel invaders.

These wars were to put great pressure on the army and the hierarchy of command. Legions had become fossilized and generally were not moved wholesale but rather provided detachments for service elsewhere when required; the reign of Marcus was the last time a whole legion was moved. Good military commanders were now required and so competent generals were promoted no matter what their status and in disregard of the normal rules, as had happened at times under the Republic. These two actions were harbingers for the future. But there was also more serious change taking place, in this case beyond the Empire.

The third and fourth centuries saw new peoples appear beyond the Empire's frontiers. Some were genuinely new, like the Huns, but others were the coalescence of the existing tribes or states into larger groups. It has been argued that this was the only way that Rome's enemies could hope to defeat the soldiers of the Empire, though the process was presumably subconscious rather than planned. The result, however, was the same, to put greater pressure on the frontier, and at a time when the Empire was weak. The building of walls round Rome by Aurelian in the 270s was a physical admission of this weakness.

Reeling under the double blows of civil war and external pressure, both Dacia (modern Transylvania) and the land between the headwaters of the Danube and the Rhine were abandoned in the 260s. Now Rome's northern frontiers were back to where they had been two hundred years before, the two great rivers.

Some emperors were strong enough to strike back. They, and others such as Gallienus, experimented with new formations. Greater emphasis was placed on the role of cavalry. Mobile armies were created with troops drawn from the frontiers. These detachments were called *vexillationes* (detachments), and this became the title of the new unit, which did not return home. There had always been an imperial bodyguard but this became more important and was now on the move with the roving emperor, and its members gained a new title, *protector*. Gallienus had a further distinction. He was the last aristocrat to rule the Empire; his successor, Claudius II was a soldier, the first of a new class of emperor, the soldier-emperor.

The reforms of Diocletian and Constantine

Diocletian's genius was to take these experiments and, rather like Augustus, create a new structure. At the top, the emperors were duplicated, Diocletian taking the eastern half and his colleague Maximian the west. Each emperor (*Augustus*) had a dedicated successor (*Caesar*), and a new capital better placed to defend the Empire. Maximian's capital was at Milan in northern Italy, Diocletian's in Nicomedia on the Sea of Marmora in western Turkey; the emperor no longer resided in Rome. Each emperor and caesar now acquired his own field army, the *comitatus*, so called as it accompanied the emperor. The frontier troops, less well paid, became the *limitanei*. Provinces were generally divided into two, with civil and military authority in each province separated. Each of thirty-three legions of Severus was duplicated, with two normally posted together on the frontier and supported by a strong cavalry force. The commanders were now professional soldiers rather than members of the aristocracy, following a career in both the civil and military service.

Constantine continued these changes, raising new legions and auxiliary units, but also disbanding the Praetorian Guard, the duties of which were assumed by his field army. The new arrangements respected reality. There is always a tension between the wish to hold a line and the need to have a mobile force available to support the front-line troops when they are attacked. Roman military dispositions now favored the latter approach. Troops remained on the frontier line and continued to deal with raiding and the like, but behind them some soldiers were placed in towns and fortified supply bases, thus denying resources to the enemy as well as acting as mobile reserves. If the invasion was serious, these troops could be supported by the mobile field armies, which would then carry the fighting into enemy territory. Defense-in-depth became the system adopted in the fourth century. Of course, nothing stands still so, in order to improve the response time, more field armies were created; that is clear in relation to Britain. Following an invasion of the Scots and Picts in 360, a small field force of four units was dispatched to Britain from the continent. In 367, a stronger body was required to deal with the next invasion. By the end of the century, a new officer had been appointed to command a field army of nine units stationed in the island.

One of our most important sources for the Roman army dates to this time. This was *The Epitome of Military Science* by Publius Flavius Vegetius Renatus, a senior officer in the Roman Civil Service. Written in the last decades of the fourth century, it is an account of the Roman army of earlier days, but is essentially a political tract in which the author seeks to persuade the emperor(s) of the day to return to the methods of those earlier years. Although therefore in some ways a lament for the past, it demonstrates a continuing interest in the success of the Roman army, and it was succeeded by treatises written in the Byzantine Empire. Obviously, it is an important source of information about the operation of the Roman army. Vegetius' military tract is not the only military book to survive from this period. A book *On Warfare* contains suggestions for new types of weapons that might help Rome regain the advantage over her enemies. The proposals indicate that the author had a fertile imagination, even though none of his ideas appears to have been put into practice.

Military architecture

The fourth century witnessed changes in military architecture. Early forts were relatively lightly defended. Tacitus had offered an explanation:

it was not expected that the forts in Germany would be attacked, since the strength of the army had been considered sufficient. Now the soldiers were better protected. New forts were altogether different from their first- and second-century predecessors. They were surrounded by high, strong walls, often equipped with bastions and with well-defended gates, the same arrangements applying to forts, fortlets, and towers. Strong supply bases were established behind the frontier, some to hold food for the frontier armies. It is not clear why the walls were so high, as Rome's enemies were generally not equipped with siege equipment.

Unfortunately, we know less about the interior of such forts and the troops who occupied them. There is disagreement about the size of late Roman regiments, though there is a general belief that they were smaller than their predecessors but precisely how much smaller is a moot point, figures ranging from half to a fifth the size of earlier regiments. Legions, 5,000 strong in the early Empire, now perhaps contained about a thousand men, while auxiliary units were about a hundred strong.

The *Notitia Dignitatum*

About the year 400, a document was prepared listing all the officials of the Roman Empire, the *Notitia Dignitatum*. This provides evidence of the military and civilian hierarchy of the Empire, clearly demonstrating, for example, that it was now divided into two parts. Most useful for students of the Roman army was the inclusion of the names of all the regiments of that army. At a glance, therefore, we can see that in Britain most of the forts along Hadrian's Wall still contained the units recorded there 200 or more years before, while in its hinterland and at some of the Saxon Shore forts along the east and south coast were new-style regiments raised in the fourth century. Two of the legions, the Second and the Sixth survived, but a field army now supplemented the army based in the island. In the first and second centuries, all troops in the province had been under the command of the governor. Now, they were divided between the command of the Duke of the Britains in the north, the Count of the

Saxon Shore in the south-east, and the Count of the Britains in charge of the field army. Interestingly, the Counts were more senior in rank to the Duke even though he had the largest force. Presumably, this reflected difference in responsibilities. Such a view might gain some support from the fact that the forts on Hadrian's Wall and in its hinterland were not upgraded to the fourth century style of military architecture; in other words, the enemy there was not as troublesome as those elsewhere. New-style military architecture is found in northern Britain, but these forts and towers were on the coast seeking to provide protection against the raids of the Scots and Picts. The overall impression given by the *Notitia*, and indeed by the military remains in Britain and by literary accounts, is that at this time, near the end of Roman Britain, the army was still a strong and formidable force.

The soldier

The changes of these years extended to all aspects of the army. We have already seen (p. 75) that it became more difficult to recruit soldiers so that greater use was made of conscription. Cities had to provide a quota of men for the army, though this might be commuted to a money payment. Some sought to evade conscription by cutting off a thumb but Constantine issued a decree stating that such men must then serve in the civil service. Some recruits came from the peoples from outside the Empire who had settled within its boundaries. Others came from beyond the frontier. There was even a return to the very early years of the Empire when men served under their own tribal leaders.

Pay and supply were also reformed. Soldiers were provided with their rations supplemented by a cash sum. The rations, and other items such as clothing, were collected in the form of taxation and passed on to the army. The middleman was the Praetorian Prefect whose staff calculated the needs of the army and arranged the level of taxation to suit. Unsurprisingly, a large bureaucracy was required to administer this system. There was also a change in accommodation. The frontier troops, the *limitanei*, continued to live in their forts, but the field armies, the *comitatenses*, were usually billeted in cities and this caused local friction, as we have already seen (p. 95).

There was greater use of heavy cavalry and this had an impact on the arms and armor of such soldiers, and often their horses, as they wore heavier armor than before. There continued to be light cavalry in the army, these soldiers sometimes being archers. Mail continued to be worn, but the tunic changed to a new style with long sleeves and patterns of decoration. Trousers were more commonly worn, and enclosed boots rather than the open sandals. The helmet style changed, though protection was retained for the nose and ears. All soldiers were equipped with the long cavalry sword and spears, though generally not as sophisticated as the earlier legionary *pilum*. Legionaries as well as auxiliaries now used throwing darts. Shields were often oval (or round) and many depicted the Christian symbol, though the *Notitia Dignitatum* demonstrates a variety of decorations.

Standards were different, too. The Christian symbol, the *chi rho*, was not only placed on the shields, but it adorned the flag (Figure 10). A new type of standard, the dragon standard, originated with cavalry units in the second century. It consisted of a bronze animal head with a tube of cloth attached so that it fluttered behind and created a whistling noise. These became much more regular throughout the army. The emperors had special dragon standards mounted on long poles and with a tube of purple cloth.

The army of the fifth century

In the late 350s, Julian was in charge of the defense of the West. In order to strengthen his army, he allowed Franks to settle within the Empire in return for military service; these soldiers became known as *foederati* from the Roman name for a treaty, *foedus*. These federates fought under their own kings. Other Germans joined the Roman army. The danger was that as the Roman army became weakened, the power of the federates would rise; Alaric who sacked Rome in 410 was one such federate leader, in his case a Visigoth. Increasingly, the new tribal groupings of Alans, Burgundians, Huns, Vandals, and Visigoths switched allegiances to suit themselves, and in the process they acquired land and in effect established kingdoms independent of Rome within the former Roman provinces. There was little of the Western Empire left when Odoacer, an army officer and probably a German, deposed the last emperor Romulus Augustulus and sent him into comfortable retirement. In the East, however, the Empire was to survive another thousand years until Constantinople fell to the Turks in 1453.

Conclusions

The Roman army developed continuously throughout its long history. Most of these changes are not recorded and we can only recognize them through observing the army at different times. Some changes were fundamental, others of simple practices. For example, Polybius recorded that the legions at Zama shouted a war cry and banged their weapons on their shields, yet by the time of the Empire several sources remarked that the legions went into battle silently.

Under Augustus, the army was a mobile fighting force, primarily formed of volunteers, with the focus on the legions. While some legions were placed to control the new provincials, many were poised to undertake new conquests. But although there were to be new conquests—Britain in 43, Dacia in 106, while Severus extended the Empire in the East and North Africa—through most of the centuries of the Empire its army occupied its time with defending what its predecessors had conquered. In effect, the army became a frontier police force, charged with preventing illicit access to the Empire. Its main task was to challenge raiders and enforce the regulations governing entry to the Empire. This is not to say that it was incapable of rising to the challenge when invasion occurred, as for example in the 170s when a couple of army units repulsed an invasion of Langobardi. But, the army became fossilized on its frontiers and the movement of whole regiments became difficult. Furthermore, if an invading army broke through the frontier, as it often did in the third century, there was no Roman defense-in-depth to stop it raiding deep into the hitherto peaceful provinces.

As a result, new arrangements were put in place. Roman cities looked to their own defense, protecting their core by the erection of strong, high walls, and this new style of military architecture was extended to the new forts constructed at the same time. In the second half of the third century, army groups, which were essentially field armies, were created and formalized as such by Diocletian and Constantine. Under Augustus there had been two main groups or grades in the provincial armies, the legions and the auxiliaries. In the late Empire there were also two grades though different than before, the *comitatenses*, the mobile field armies, and the *limitatenses*, the frontier armies. In other ways, the army responded to the requirements of the time, making greater use of heavy cavalry. Its ability to reinvent itself was one of the reasons behind the long success of the Roman army.

It is not surprising that we have a rose-tinted view of the Roman army. It was a formidable fighting force, well trained, well disciplined, well armed, and used to winning battles. In fact, it lost many battles, often through the incompetence of its generals. Its officers could be harsh disciplinarians, operating in the manner described by Polybius and Tacitus. But the soldiers could also behave badly. On the death of Augustus, two armies mutinied (even one of Caesar's legions had mutinied). There are several references to soldiers deserting to the enemy. Drunkenness is also recorded on quite a few occasions. One of the problems was the very success of the Roman state. For many years, Roman soldiers had little to do. In such circumstances, they became lax, as Tacitus so memorably described the soldiers on the eastern frontier: soldiers who had never been on watch, who had never worn a breastplate. Tacitus may have been exaggerating the situation, but there must have been some truth in it. And we have seen that they could be corrupt. Yet this remained a victorious army over many centuries, one of the most successful armies the world has seen.

Glossary

Centurion the officer in charge of a century of 80 infantry.

Cataphracts heavy armed cavalry.

Comitatenses the general name for the field armies of the late Empire.

Contubernium a barrack-room group of, usually, eight men.

Decurion the officer in charge of a troop of 30 or 32 men.

Equestrian the lower order of aristocracy.

Legate originally the deputy of a senior officer; in the Empire, the title of a governor or the commander of a legion.

Limitanei the frontier troops of the late Empire.

Phalanx the formation used by the Macedonian army of heavy infantry wielding long spears.

Prefect the commander of a body of men, including auxiliary units.

Senator a member of the senate, the senior order of aristocracy.

Tribune an officer in the legion or the commander of a thousand-strong auxiliary unit.

Vexillation a detachment so called because it marched behind a *vexillum* (a flag).

Select List of Roman Emperors

Augustus	30 BC to AD 14
Tiberius	14–37
Gaius (Caligula)	37–41
Claudius	41–54
Nero	54–68
Vespasian	69–79
Titus	79–81
Domitian	81–96
Nerva	96–98
Trajan	98–117
Hadrian	117–138
Antoninus Pius	138–161
Marcus Aurelius	161–180
Commodus	180–192
Septimius Severus	193–211
Caracalla	211–217
Elagabalus	218–222
Severus Alexander	222–235
Gallienus	253–268
Aurelian	270–275
Diocletian (East)	284–305
Maximian (West)	286–305
Constantius I (West)	305–306
Constantine I	306–337
Constantius II	337–361
Julian	361–363
Valentinian I	364–375
Valeus	364–378
Theodosius I	379–395
Honorius (West)	395–423
Arcadius (East)	395–408

Suggestions for Further Study

Julius Caesar's account of the Gallic War is the best description of the Roman army in action in the late Republic, while Ammianus Marcellinus offers a valuable insight into the late Roman army's activities; both written by army officers.

Julius Agricola's biography was written by his son-in-law, the Roman historian Tacitus. It is a good place to begin a study of the careers of senior Roman officers.

The Vindolanda writing tables offer intimate details of life on the British frontier at the beginning of the second century.

The military treatises by Arrian, Polybius, pseudo-Hyginus, and Vegetius have all been published, the first three by Ares Publishers and the last by Liverpool University Press.

Arrian's voyage to inspect the Roman military bases round the Black Sea, the *Periplus Ponti Euxini*, is published by the Bristol Classical Press; it is a polished account of what we presume was an everyday aspect of army life.

Visible Roman military sites are spread across the landscape of Britain from Derbyshire to central Scotland as well as along the south and east coasts. A useful guide to what can be seen is Roger J. A. Wilson (2002), *A Guide to the Roman Remains in Britain*, London: Constable, 4th edition. The guidebook also contains a list of museums containing Roman objects.

Inscriptiones Latinae Selectae, abbreviated ILS, is a selection of Latin inscriptions: Dessau, H. (1892–1916) *Inscriptiones Latinae Selectae*, 3 Volumes, Berlin: Weidmann.

Further Reading

Ancient sources

Ammianus Marcellinus, *History of the Roman Empire* (written in the late
   fourth century)
   Translations: Rolfe, J. C. (1950) *Ammianus Marcellinus: History*, London:
   Loeb; Hamilton, W. (1986) *Ammianus Marcellinus: The Later Roman
   Empire (A.D. 354–378)*, Harmondsworth: Penguin.
Anonymus, *de rebus bellicis* (probably written about 368)
   Translation: Ireland, R. (1979) *De rebus bellicis*, Oxford: BAR International
   Series 63.
Arrian, *Circumnavigation of the Black Sea* (written in the 130s)
   Translation: Liddle, A. (2003) *Arrian, Periplus Ponti Euxini*, London:
   Duckworth.
Arrian, *The Expedition against the Alans* (written in the 130s)
   Translation: DeVoto, J. G. (1993) *FLAVIUS ARRIANUS, ΤΕΧΝΗ ΤΑΚΤΙΚΑ
   (Tactical Handbook) and "ΕΚΤΑΞΙΣ ΚΑΤΑ ᾽ΑΛΑΝΩΝ (The Expedition
   against the Alans)*, Chicago, IL: Aries.
Caesar, *The Gallic War* (describing the conquest of Gaul in the 50s BCE)
   Translations: Edwards, H. J. (1917) *Caesar: The Gallic War*, London: Loeb;
   Handford, S. A. (1951) *Caesar: The Conquest of Gaul*, Harmondsworth:
   Penguin.
Caesar, *The Alexandrian, African and Spanish Wars* (accounts of Caesar's wars
   but written after his death)
   Translation: Way, A. G. (1955) *Alexandrian War. African War. Spanish War*,
   London: Loeb.
Cassius Dio, *A History of Rome* (written in the first quarter of the third
   century)
   Translation: Cary, E. (1925) *Dio Cassius: Roman History*, London: Loeb.
Frontinus, *Stratagems* (written in the late first century)
   Translation: Bennett, C. E. (1925) *Frontinus, Stratagems and Aqueducts*,
   London: Loeb.
Herodian, *A History of Rome* (written about 248)
   Translation: Whittaker, C. R. (1969) *Herodian: History of the Empire*,
   London: Loeb.

Historia Augusta: Lives of the Later Emperors (written in the fourth century)
   Translations: Magie, D. (1921-32) *Historia Augusta*, London: Loeb; Birley,
   A. R. (1976) *Lives of the Later Caesars*, Harmondsworth: Penguin.
Lucan, *Pharsalia, Dramatic Episodes of the Civil Wars* (written during the
   reign of Nero)
   Translations: Duff, J. D. (1928) *The Civil War (Pharsalia)*, London: Loeb;
   Graves, R. (1956) *Pharsalia*, Harmondsworth: Penguin; Braund, S. F.
   (1992) *Civil War*, Oxford: Oxford University Press.
Josephus, *The Jewish War* (written in 75–79)
   Translations: Thackerey, H. St. J. (1925–28) *Josephus: The Jewish War*,
   London: Loeb; Williamson, G. A. (1969) *Josephus: The Jewish War*,
   Harmondsworth: Penguin.
Plutarch, *Roman Lives* (written in the late first century)
   Translations: Various authors, *Lives* (11 volumes), London: Loeb; Warner, R.
   (1958) *Fall of the Roman Republic*, Harmondsworth: Penguin;
   Waterfield, R. (1999) *Plutarch, Roman Lives* (8 lives), Oxford: Oxford
   University Press.
Polybius (written in the late second century BC)
   Translations: Scott-Kilvert, I. (1979) *Polybius: The Rise of the Roman
   Empire*, Harmondsworth: Penguin; Paton, W. R. (2010–12) *The Histories*
   (6 volumes), London: Loeb.
Pseudo-Hyginus (probably written in the fourth century)
   Translation: Miller, M. C. J and DeVoto, J. G. (1994) *Polybius and Pseudo-
   Hyginus: The Fortification of the Roman Camp*, Chicago, IL: Ares.
Tacitus, *The Life of Agricola* and *Germania* (published in 98)
   Translations: Page, T. E. (1914) *Tacitus: Dialogues, Agricola and Germania*,
   London: Loeb; Birley, A. R. (1999) *Tacitus, Agricola and Germany*,
   Harmondsworth: Penguin.
Tacitus, *The Annals* (published in 116)
   Translations: Jackson, J. (1931) *Annals*, London: Loeb; Grant, E. (1959)
   Tacitus, The Annals of Imperial Rome, Harmondsworth: Penguin;
   Yardley, J. C. (2008) *The Annals*, Oxford: Oxford University Press.
Tacitus, *The Histories* (written in 104–109)
   Translations: Moore, C. H. (1925 and 1931) *Tacitus: The Histories*, London:
   Loeb; Wellesley, K. (1964) *Tacitus: The Histories*, Harmondsworth:
   Penguin.
Three Byzantine Military Treatises (dating to the sixth and the tenth
   centuries)

Translation: Dennis, G. T. (1985) *Three Byzantine Military Treatises*, Washington, DC: Dumbarton Oaks.

Vegetius, *Epitome of military science* (written in the late fourth century) Translation: Milner, N. P. (1993) *Vegetius: Epitome of Military Science*, Liverpool: Liverpool University Press.

Military documents

Birley, A. R. (2002) *Garrison Life at Vindolanda*, Stroud: Tempus.

Bowman, A. K. (1994) *Life and Letters on the Roman Frontier*, London: British Museum.

Bowman, A. K. and Thomas, J. D. (1994) *The Vindolanda Writing-tablets (Tabulae Vindolandenses II)*; (2003) *The Vindolanda Writing-tablets (Tabulae Vindolandenses III)*, London: British Museum.

Campbell, B. (1994) *The Roman Army 31 BC – AD 337: A Source Book*, London: Routledge.

Fink, R. O. (1971) *Roman Military Records on Papyrus*, Cleveland, OH: Case Western Reserve University Press.

Speidel, M. P. (2006) *Emperor Hadrian's Speeches to the African Army: A New Text*, Mainz: Verlag des Römisch-Germanischen Zentralmuseums.

Tomlin, R. S. O. (1998) "Roman manuscripts from Carlisle: the ink-written tablets", *Britannia* 29, 31–84.

Sculpture

Ferris, I. (2009) *Hate and War: The Column of Marcus Aurelius*, Stroud: History Press.

Keppie, L. (1998) *Roman Inscribed and Sculptured Stones in the Hunterian Museum, University of Glasgow*, London: Britannia Monograph Series 13.

Lepper, F. and Frere, S. (1988) *Trajan's Column*, Gloucester: Alan Sutton.

The Roman army

Austin, N. J. E. and Rankov, N. B. (1995) *Exploratio: Military and Political Intelligence in the Roman World from the Second Punic War to the Battle of Adrianople*, London: Routledge.

Campbell, B. (2002) *War and Society in Imperial Rome 31* BC – AD *284*, London: Routledge.

Campbell, D. B. (2013) *The Rise of Imperial Rome*, Oxford: Osprey.

Campbell, J. B. (1984) *The Emperor and the Roman Army*, Oxford: Clarendon Press.

Connolly, P. (1975) *The Roman Army*, London: Macdonald Educational.

Connolly, P. (1981) *Greece and Rome at War*, London: Macdonald.

Connolly, P. (1988) *Tiberius Claudius Maximus, The Cavalryman*, Oxford: Oxford University Press.

Connolly, P. (1988) *Tiberius Claudius Maximus, The Legionary*, Oxford: Oxford University Press.

Davies, R. W. (1989) *Service in the Roman Army*, edited by Breeze, D. J. and Maxfield, V. A., Edinburgh: Edinburgh University Press.

Dobson, M. (2008) *The Roman Army of the Republic: The Second Century* BC, *Polybius and the Camps at Numantia, Spain*, Oxford: Oxbow.

Fischer, T. (2012) *Die Armee der Caesaren, Archäologie und Geschichte*, Regensburg: Friedrich Pustet.

Gilliver, K., Goldsworthy, A. and Whitby, M. (2005) *Rome at War: Caesar and his Legacy*, Oxford: Osprey.

Goldsworthy, A. (2000) *Roman Warfare*, London: Cassell.

Goldsworthy, A. (2003) *The Complete Roman Army*, London: Thames & Hudson.

Goldsworthy, A. and Haynes, I., eds. (1999) "The Roman Army as a Community in Peace and War", *Journal of Roman Archaeology Supplementary Series* 34.

Hanson, W. S., ed. (2009) "The Army and Frontiers of Rome", *Journal of Roman Archaeology Supplementary Series* 74.

Holder, P. A. (1982) *The Roman Army in Britain*, London: Batsford.

Hyland, A. (1990) *Equus: The Horse in the Roman World*, London: Batsford.

Hyland, A. (1993) *Training the Roman Cavalry from Arrian's Ars Tactica*, Stroud: Alan Sutton.

Isaac, B. (1990) *The Limits of Empire: The Roman Army in the East*, Oxford: Oxford University Press.

James, S. (2011) *Rome & the Sword: How Warriors and Weapons Shaped Roman History*, London: Thames & Hudson.

Keppie, L. J. F. (1998) *The Making of the Roman Army: From Republic to Empire*, London: Batsford.

Le Bohec, Y. (1994) *The Imperial Roman Army*, London: Routledge.

Lee, A. D. (1993) *Information & Frontiers: Roman Foreign Relations in Late Antiquity*, Cambridge: Cambridge University Press.

Mattern, S. P. (1999) *Rome and the Enemy: Imperial Strategy in the Principate*, Berkeley, CA: University of California Press.

Maxfield, V. A. (1981) *The Military Decorations of the Roman Army*, London: Batsford.

Phang, S. E. (2008) *Roman Military Service: Ideologies of Discipline in the Late Republic and Early Principate*, New York: Cambridge University Press.

Roth, J. P. (1999) *The Logistics of the Roman Army at War (264 BC – AD 235)*, Leiden: Brill.

Southern, P. (2007) *The Roman Army: A Social and Institutional History*, Oxford: Oxford University Press.

Southern, P. and Dixon, K. R. (1996) *The Late Roman Army*, London: Batsford.

Watson, G. R. (1969) *The Roman Soldier*, London: Thames & Hudson.

Webster, G. (1985) *The Roman Imperial Army*, 3rd edn., London: A. & C. Black.

Branches of the army

Baillie Reynolds, P. K. (1926) *The Vigiles of Imperial Rome*, London: Oxford University Press.

Bingham, S. (2013) *The Praetorian Guard: A History of Rome's Elite Special Forces*, London: I. B. Tauris & Co.

Cheesman, G. L. (1914) *The Auxilia of the Roman Imperial Army*, Oxford: Clarendon Press.

Haynes, I. (2013) *Blood of the Provinces: The Roman Auxilia and the Making of Provincial Society from Augustus to the Severans*, Oxford: Oxford University Press.

Parker, H. M. D. (1928) *The Roman Legions*, London: Heffer.

Rankov, B. (1994) *The Praetorian Guard*, Oxford: Osprey.

Saddington, D. B. (1982) *The Development of the Roman Auxiliary Forces from Caesar to Vespasian*, Harare: University of Zimbabwe.

Speidel, M. (1978) *Guards of the Roman Armies*, Bonn: Rudolf Habelt.

The navy

Mason, D. J. P. (2003) *Roman Britain and the Roman Navy*, Stroud: Tempus.

Pitassi, M. (2009) *The Navies of Rome*, Woodbridge: Boydell.

Reddé, M. (1986) *Mare Nostrum*, Paris.

Starr, C. G. (1960) *The Roman Imperial Navy, 31 B.C. – A.D. 324*, 2nd edn. Cambridge: Cambridge University Press.

Military installations

Allison, P. M. (2013) *People and Spaces in Roman Military Bases*, Cambridge: Cambridge University Press.

Bidwell, P. T. (2007) *The Roman Fort*, Stroud: Tempus.

Bishop, M. C. (2012) *Handbook to Roman Legionary Fortresses*, Barnsley: Pen & Sword.

Breeze, D.J. (2007) *Roman Frontiers in Britain*, London: Bloomsbury.

Breeze, D. J. (2011) *The Frontiers of Imperial Rome*, Barnsley: Pen & Sword.

Connolly, P. (1991) *The Roman Fort*, Oxford: Oxford University Press.

Johnson, A. (1983) *Roman Forts*, London: A. & C. Black.

Johnson, S. (1983) *Late Roman Fortifications*, London: Batsford.

Jones, R. H. (2012) *Roman Camps in Britain*, Stroud: Amberley.

Lander, J. (1984) *Roman Stone Fortifications: Variations and Change from the First Century A.D. to the Fourth*, Oxford: BAR International Series 206.

Whittaker, C. R. (2004) *Rome and its Frontiers: The Dynamics of Empire*, London: Johns Hopkins University Press.

Woolliscroft, D. J. (2001) *Roman Military Signalling*, Stroud: Tempus.

Equipment

Bishop, M. C. and Coulson, J. C. N. (2006) *Roman Military Equipment from the Punic Wars to the Fall of Rome*, Oxford: Oxbow.

Breeze, D. J. and Bishop, M. C., eds (2013) *The Crosby Garrett Helmet*, Pewsey: The Armatura Press.

Campbell, D. B. (2003) *Greek and Roman Artillery 399 BC – AD 363*, Oxford: Osprey.

Feugère, M. (1993) *Weapons of the Romans*, Stroud: Tempus.

Sumner, G. (2009) *Roman Military Dress*, Stroud: The History Press.

Wilkins, A. (2003) *Roman Artillery*, Princes Risborough: Shire.

The enemy

Burns, T. (2003) *Rome and the Barbarians 100 B.C. – A.D. 400*, Baltimore, MD: Johns Hopkins University Press.

Ferris, I. M. (2000) *Enemies of Rome: Barbarians through Roman Eyes*, Stroud: Sutton.

Millar, F. 1966 *The Roman Empire and its Neighbours*, London: Weidenfeld & Nicolson.

Wells, P. S. (1999) *The Barbarians Speak: How the Conquered Peoples Shaped Roman Europe*, Princeton, NJ: Princeton University Press.

Battles and sieges

Campbell, D. B. (2003) *Greek and Roman Siege Machinery 399 BC – AD 363*, Oxford: Osprey.

Campbell, D. B. (2005) *Siege Warfare in the Roman World 146 BC – AD 378*, Oxford: Osprey.

Campbell, D. B. (2010) *Mons Graupius AD 83*, Oxford: Osprey.

Cowan, R. (2007) *Roman Battle Tactics 109 BC – AD 313*, Oxford: Osprey.

Davies, G. (2006) *Roman Siege Works*, Stroud: Tempus.

Gilliver, K. (1999) *The Roman Art of War*, Stroud: Tempus.

Goldsworthy, A. (1996) *The Roman Army at War 100 BC – AD 200*, Oxford: Clarendon Press.

Goldsworthy, A. (2001) *Cannae*, London: Phoenix.

Maxwell, G. (1990) *A Battle Lost: Romans and Caledonians at Mons Graupius*, Edinburgh: Edinburgh University Press.

Roth, J. P. (2009) *Roman Warfare*, Cambridge: Cambridge University Press.

Osprey has a large portfolio of books on different aspects of the Roman army, all well illustrated and written by specialists in the field.

The *Frontiers of the Roman Empire* series of popular guides.

A series of multi-language guides, many of which are available on line at www. limes-oesterreich.at, include:

Breeze, D. J. (2009) *The Antonine Wall*, Edinburgh.

Breeze, D. J. (2011) *Hadrian's Wall*, Hexham.

Dyczek, P. (2008) *The Lower Danube Limes in Bulgaria*, Warsaw/Vienna.

Harmadyová, K., Rajtár, J. and Schmidtová, J. (2008) *Slovakia*, Nitra.

Jilek, S. (2009) *The Danube Limes: A Roman River Frontier*, Warsaw.

Jilek, S., Kuttner, E. and Schwarcz, A. (2011) *The Danube Limes in Österreich*, Wien.

Mattingly, D., Rushworth, A., Sterry, M. and Leitch, V. (2013) *The African Frontiers*, Edinburgh.

Visy, Z. (2008, 2011) *The Roman Limes in Hungary*, Pécs.

Index

Actium, battle of 69
Adamklissi xiii, 9
Adrianople, battle of 68–9
Africa 3, 10, 17, 23, 24, 39, 51, 53, 74,
    88, 95, 116, 117, 118, 131, 146
Agricola, governor 44, 49, 51, 56, 64–5,
    137
Alamanni, people 67–8, 75, 124
Alans, people 5, 53, 72
Albano, legionary base 32, 39
allies 16, 22, 24, 30–1, 45, 61
Ammianus Marcellinus, historian 6,
    43, 67–8, 71, 72, 119, 137, 139
Antioch, city 28, 37
Antonine Wall xiii, 9, 10, 66, 84, 103,
    112, 117, 118, 145
Antoninus Pius, emperor 3, 9, 135
archers 24, 31, 32, 45, 59, 64, 67, 69,
    101, 129
Armenia, kingdom 43, 57, 143
armor 15, 19, 23, 49, 61, 63, 90, 91,
    101–5, 107, 108, 113, 118, 129, 132
Arrian, governor and writer 5, 53, 72,
    88, 90, 135, 137, 139, 142
artillery 25, 47, 58, 70, 72, 87, 89, 96,
    107, 144
Augustus, emperor 1, 4, 5, 20, 26,
    27, 28, 30, 32, 33, 41, 50–1, 57, 60,
    61–2, 69, 73, 74, 77, 91, 100, 101,
    112, 123, 125, 127, 131, 132, 135,
    143
auxilia/auxiliary units 1–2, 8, 25, 30–2,
    36, 37, 45, 64, 65, 72, 73, 74, 77, 78,
    80, 90, 91, 92, 100, 101, 104, 105,
    108, 132, 133, 143

baggage 21–2, 45, 46, 47
barrack-blocks 22, 84, 115, 116, 133
Batavians 31, 32, 87, 91
bath house 85, 86

battles 4, 12, 18–19, 25, 26, 41, 57–70,
    131, 145
battle formation 17, 20, 23, 54–5, 58,
    59, 62, 64, 65, 67, 68
Bearsden, fort 84, 85, 86, 112
Bible 94, 96
Black Sea 5, 90, 137, 139
boots 78, 102, 107, 129
Britain 31, 34, 36, 39, 43, 44, 48, 49, 51,
    56, 62–5, 73, 85, 99, 100, 113, 118,
    119, 126, 127–8, 131
building 111–19

Caesar, see Julius Caesar
Caledonia/Caledonians 44, 56–7,
    64–5, 67, 145
Caligula, emperor 93, 135
camp followers 3, 47, 61
campaigning season 20, 49, 111
camps xiii, 10, 21, 22–3, 44, 45, 47–9,
    55, 61, 64, 71, 72, 79, 89, 111–12
Cannae, battle of 18, 56, 69, 145
Cappadocia, province 5, 82, 88, 107
Caracalla, emperor 41–2, 77, 135
Caratacus, British general 62–3, 66
careers, military 19, 32, 35, 37–9,
    96–100
Carlisle, fort 6, 86–7, 141
Carrhae, battle of 55, 58
Carthage 17–19, 53, 57, 69
Cassius Dio, historian 5, 61, 62, 64, 67,
    139
cavalry 2, 15, 16, 19, 20, 24, 30, 36, 43,
    44, 45, 58, 59, 60, 63, 64, 66, 67, 69,
    75, 77, 85, 99, 104, 106, 108, 109,
    125, 129, 132, 142
centurion 1, 2, 3, 20, 30, 33, 34, 45, 49,
    54, 59, 91, 94, 96, 97, 98, 99, 101,
    107, 133
century 2, 15, 20, 23, 84, 118

civil wars 24, 26, 54, 69–70, 124
Claudius, emperor 35, 73, 77, 90, 123
Claudius Pompeianus, general 37–8, 53
cloaks 82, 101–2, 105, 108
clothing 80, 81, 82, 101–2, 104, 107, 108, 129, 144
clubmen 31, 104, 105
cohort 2, 20, 23, 36, 59, 65, 72, 78, 79, 80, 81, 90–1, 107, 108, 109, 116, 118
Commodus, emperor xiii, 39, 53, 135
Constantine, emperor 56, 57, 60, 69, 75, 123, 125, 128, 132, 135
consuls 16, 19, 22, 23, 98
cooking 46, 47, 84, 92
corruption 33, 68, 93–6
crest, see plume
Ctesiphon, Parthian capital 57, 59

Dacia/Dacians xiii, 4, 9, 29, 37, 53, 73, 93
dagger 101, 102, 104
Dalmatia, province 28, 41
Danube, river xiii, 28, 32, 33, 35, 36, 37, 67, 73, 88, 145, 146
decorations 20, 22, 90–1, 143
decurion 97, 133
deployment 8, 27–8, 36, 37, 73–4, 125–6
Dio, see Cassius Dio
Diocletian, emperor 4, 107, 123, 125, 132, 135
diploma 7–8
Domitian, emperor 36, 77, 78, 91, 120, 135
Domitius Corbulo, general 57, 73, 90
drink 47, 50, 85
Dura, city 43, 71–2, 79, 80, 81, 88
duties, peacetime 73, 80–1, 87–90, 96–7, 131

Egypt, province xvi, 6, 28, 50, 76, 78, 79, 81, 82, 83, 85, 92, 93, 95, 107, 108
Euphrates, river 28, 43, 57, 116
exploration 44, 50–1

factories, weapons 23, 107
families 3, 20, 35, 78, 92–3
field armies 4, 125, 126, 129, 131–2, 133
flags 21, 26, 47, 56, 59, 90, 129, 133
fleet, see navy
food 42–3, 45–6, 50, 51, 78, 80, 81, 82, 84–5, 86, 100
foraging 41, 43, 111
forts 3, 10, 36, 37, 55, 73, 78, 84, 86–7, 90, 107, 112–16, 120, 126–9, 131, 143
frontiers 2, 37, 73, 75, 87–8, 116–17, 124, 126, 127, 129, 131, 132, 142, 143, 144, 145

Gallienus, emperor 124, 125, 135
Gaul/s 16, 23, 24, 31, 42, 43, 53, 62, 107, 112, 116
German frontier/*limes* 10, 75, 117, 118
Germanicus, general 35, 42, 43, 51, 55, 62
Germany 29, 31, 35, 42, 55, 61–2, 74, 75, 78, 90, 91, 116, 124, 126, 127
gladius, see sword
governors of provinces 3, 87, 90, 95, 97, 99, 100, 109, 126, 133
Greece/Greeks 15, 19, 20, 23, 24, 53, 72, 117

Hadrian 1, 4, 5, 27, 32, 41, 74, 90, 92, 94, 95, 108, 116–17, 135, 141
Hadrian's Wall 7, 10, 81, 111–12, 117, 118, 119, 120, 127–8, 145
Hannibal 17–19, 56, 57, 88
health 50, 71, 80, 85–7
helmets 47, 63, 79, 89, 90, 101, 102–4, 108, 113, 117, 129, 144
horses 16, 41, 42, 44, 66, 80, 92, 101, 104, 106, 109, 129, 142
hospital 82, 85, 87, 115

infantry 1, 2, 15, 16, 19, 30, 36, 84 see also legions
inscriptions 8–10, 93, 113, 118, 120, 135

javelin 16, 20, 23, 54, 60, 65, 103, 129
Jerusalem, siege of 70–1, 103
Josephus, historian 5, 44, 45, 53, 73, 140
Judaea 36, 53, 61, 70–1, 82, 100, 107
Julian, emperor 43, 44, 45, 57, 67–8, 129, 135
Julius Caesar, 5, 24–6, 28, 41, 42, 45, 53, 55, 56, 59–60, 70, 71, 77, 105, 112, 116, 132, 137, 139, 142, 143

latrine 84, 85, 86–7
leave 82, 91–2
legate 2, 30, 98, 133
legions 1–2, 9, 16, 17, 19, 22, 23, 24, 26, 27, 28, 29, 30, 32, 33, 35, 36, 37, 41, 44, 45, 49, 54, 55, 58, 59, 61, 64, 67, 73, 75, 76, 77, 81, 91, 97, 98, 99, 101, 103, 105, 113, 118, 119, 1120, 123, 124, 125, 127, 129, 131, 132, 133, 143, 144
length of service 15, 16, 19, 20, 30, 33, 100
line of battle; see battle formation
Livy, historian 5, 17, 20
location of legions 28, 37

Machaerus, siege of xiii, 10, 70
maniple 20
march, order of 22, 44–5, 54, 61
Marcus Aurelius, emperor xiii, 4, 37, 53, 77, 123, 124, 135, 141
Marius, Gaius, general 23, 24
Mark Antony, general 26, 27, 58, 60, 69
marriage 3, 20, 78, 92–3
Masada, siege of xiii, 10, 70, 71
medical matters 47, 85, 96 see also health
mines 71–2, 87
Mons Graupius, battle of 64–5, 145
mutinies 33, 77, 132

navy 2–3, 7, 17, 18, 19, 33, 43, 51, 69–70, 76, 77, 99, 143, 144

Nero, emperor 33, 36, 49, 57, 59, 135, 140
North Sea 43, 51, 62, 94
Notitia Dignitatum 8, 107, 127–8, 129
Numantia, siege works xiii, 10, 11, 22, 47, 70, 93, 111, 142
numerus 2

oath, military 76, 78, 80, 88
officers 1–2, 16, 20, 32, 35, 37, 39, 43, 65, 69, 76, 80, 85, 90, 95, 97–100, 105, 118, 125, 127, 133, 137
optio 20, 54, 97, 120

Pannonia, province(s) 28, 33, 41, 124
parades 77, 80, 84, 88, 101
Parthia/Parthians 4, 28, 39, 41–2, 58–9, 73, 123, 124
pay 16, 30, 39, 77–8, 88, 100, 108, 109, 128
Persia 43, 57, 71
phalanx 15–16, 133
Pharsalus, battle of 26, 59
Philippi, battle of 60
pilum see javelin
Pliny the Younger, writer 75, 76, 88, 105
plumes 20, 103, 107
Plutarch, historian 44
Polybius, historian 5, 19, 22, 46, 47, 49, 81, 131, 132, 137, 140
Pompey, general 26, 42, 59–60, 70
Praetorian Guard 3, 32, 35, 39, 50, 75, 99, 100, 105, 125, 143
prefect 17, 95, 99, 109, 128, 133
prefect of the camp 1, 98, 99, 119
promotion 96–100, 124
pseudo-Hyginus, author 6, 47, 49, 111, 112, 137, 140
Punic Wars: see Carthage
punishments 21, 33–5, 91

rebellions 5, 28–30, 35–6, 61, 63–4, 70–1, 78, 91
reconnaissance 44

records 6–7, 76, 79, 80–3, 97
recruitment 15, 19–20, 24, 31, 35, 74–8, 98, 128, 129
Republic, Roman 5, 15–26, 30–1, 53, 54, 73, 74, 111, 112, 124, 142
retirement 7, 85, 92, 100
Rhine, river 4, 28, 33, 35, 36, 37, 61, 62, 67–8, 73, 74, 116, 118
roads 16, 79, 115, 116, 122
role of army 1–3, 73, 88, 126, 131
Rome xiii, 3, 15, 32, 33, 74, 79, 80, 98, 123, 124, 129

sailors 17, 108 see also navy
Scipio Aemilianus 19, 22, 93
Scipio Africanus 17, 18–19, 23, 47, 54, 57, 60, 70
scouts/scouting 44, 45, 61, 141
Septimius Severus, emperor 32, 39, 49, 53, 67, 77, 92, 115, 123, 125, 131, 135
Severus Alexander, emperor, 39, 45, 123, 124, 135
shield 15, 16, 47, 61, 65, 101, 103, 104, 106, 107, 108, 113, 117, 129
sieges/siege works xiii, 10, 22, 24–5, 26, 45, 57, 70–2, 145
size of the army 1, 27, 41, 125, 127
slaves 75, 76, 87, 92, 95
slingers 24, 59, 89, 104, 105
Spain 18, 20, 23, 24, 28, 31, 37, 44, 74, 85
spear 15, 20, 66, 71, 79, 107, 117, 129, 133
standards/standard bearers 29, 45, 55–6, 67, 68, 78, 83, 87, 97, 101, 105, 129
Strasbourg, battle of 67–8
strategy 56–7, 143
Suetonius Paulinus, general 51, 63–4
supply/ies 41–4, 51, 56, 77, 82, 87, 101, 107, 121, 126, 127, 128
sword 15, 54, 65, 69, 79, 96, 103–4, 109, 129, 142
symbols, legionary 28, 29
Syria, province 6, 31, 109

Tacitus, historian 5, 33, 44, 56, 62–5, 77, 90, 126–7, 132, 137, 140
taxes 30, 87, 93, 94–5, 128
tents 42, 46, 47, 49, 79, 108
Teutoberg Forest, battle of 61–2, 101
Tiberius, emperor 28, 32, 33–5, 41, 57, 62, 74, 135
Titus, emperor 70, 77, 135
tools 56, 119, 121–2
tortoise formation 62, 63, 70
towers 10, 22, 71, 72, 116, 117, 119, 127, 128
training 18, 23, 74, 79–80, 88–90, 96
Trajan, emperor 4, 37, 38, 72, 73, 88, 113, 115, 116, 123, 135
Trajan's Column xiii, 9, 29, 31, 38, 42, 46, 47, 104, 105, 106, 113, 117, 141
transport 42, 45–7, 87, 92
tribune 16, 19, 20, 35, 98, 99, 133
trumpets/trumpeters 55, 59, 67, 68, 87, 96
Turin, battle of 60

Urban Cohorts 3, 32

Valu lui Traian, frontier 10, 117
Valens, emperor 68–9, 135
Valentinian, emperor 119, 135
Varus, governor 55, 61, 67, 74, 91
Vegetius, writer 6, 41, 47, 69, 72, 75, 101, 111, 112, 125, 137, 141
Vespasian, emperor 36, 45, 70, 77, 135, 143
Vigiles 3, 32, 99, 143
Vindolanda writing tablets xiii, 6, 7, 81–2, 84, 85, 92, 95–6, 104, 118, 137, 141

weapons 12, 15, 19, 47, 65, 101, 107, 108, 142, 144
wills 77, 78, 108
wives 3, 35, 92–3, 95, 100

Zama, battle of 17, 18–19, 60, 131